MW01282416

CEO Boot Camp

Frameworks and Insights from 15 Years of

CEO Connection CEO Boot Camps

George Bradt

GHP Press

Copyright © 2019 by George Bradt. All rights reserved.

No part of this publication may be reproduced, stored in a retrieval system, or transmitted in any form or by any means, electronic, mechanical, photocopying, recording, scanning, or otherwise, except as permitted under Section 107 or 108 of the 1976 United States Copyright Act, without either the prior written permission of the Publisher, or authorization through payment of the appropriate per-copy fee to the Copyright Clearance Center, 222 Rosewood Drive, Danvers, MA 01923, (978) 750-8400, fax (978) 646-8600, or on the web at www.copyright.com. Requests to the publisher for permission should be addressed to gbradt@primegenesis.com at GHP Press.

Limit of Liability/Disclaimer of Warranty: While the publisher and author have used their best efforts in preparing this book, they make no representations or warranties with the respect to the accuracy or completeness of the contents of this book and specifically disclaim any implied warranties of merchantability or fitness for a particular purpose. No warranty may be created or extended by sales representatives or written sales materials. The advice and strategies contained herein may not be suitable for your situation. You should consult with a professional where appropriate. Neither the publisher nor the author shall be liable for damages arising herefrom.

Since 2005, CEO Connection's CEO Boot Camps have brought together 8-12 mid-market CEOs and outside experts at a time to spend a day discussing ways to scale through points of inflection. Those boot camps have helped evolve thinking on frameworks for leadership and provided insights into ways to implement them.

This book lays out those frameworks and insights to help you improve your own leadership as a CEO.

We do not name any of the CEOs in the room as confidentiality is one of the hallmarks of the boot camps. This allows you to get the benefit of unvarnished, raw thinking by some smart, experienced leaders – your peers - as shared in an open, trusting environment where the real stuff gets discussed on relevant leadership topics.

Every organization goes through points of inflection. Successfully leading through them requires CEOs to recognize events that change the way they think and act – generally changes in situation or ambitions – and then change their strategy, organization, and the way they lead and operate all together, all at the same time, in sync to avoid breaking the system as they accelerate through turning points.

To that end, we begin with a relatively brief overview and "best of" section and then dig into five boot camp modules for those that want more. Those module sections include some of the stories I share in the boot camps – many pulled from my Forbes articles.

Module: **"Best of"** the CEO Boot Camps (p7)

Acknowledgements, about the author and references follow those.

"Best of" the CEO Boot Camps – core insights & frameworks

Reflecting back on the 15 years of CEO Connection CEO Boot Camps and re-reading the summary notes yields this highly subjective view of the most important insights. We don't take notes during the boot camps, but we do end each boot camp by asking the CEOs present three questions:

1. What are you going to do differently tomorrow?
2. What was most valuable?
3. How can we make these boot camps even more valuable?

Module 1: Scaling up through a point of inflection

The #1 job of a CEO is to own the vision and values – purpose. CEOs at CEO Boot Camps get that. It is about inspiring and enabling. Not surprisingly, a lot of what people say they are going to do differently relates to vision, values and culture.

BRAVE Leadership Framework

Leadership is about inspiring and enabling others to do their absolute best together to realize a meaningful and rewarding shared purpose.

Environment - Where to play? (Context)
 Organizational History | Recent Results | Conditional Scenarios
Values - What matters and why? (Purpose)
 Mission | Vision | Guiding Principles
Attitudes - How to win? (Choices)
 Strategy | Priorities | Culture
Relationships - How to connect? (Communication)
 Specialized | Hierarchy | Matrix | Decentralized | (Portfolio)
Behaviors - What impact? (Implementation)
 Freeing Support | Command & Control |
 Shared Responsibility | Guided Accountability

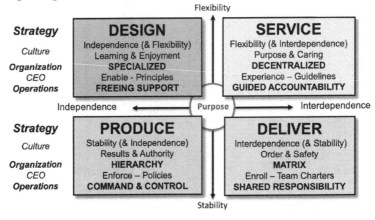

1. **Assess** the changes in your situation or ambition. *What* has changed? *So what* are the implications of that? *Now what* must you do? If the answer is nothing new, fine. If the answer is to continue to evolve, fine. But if the answer is to accelerate through an inflection point, go on to the next step.

2. **Strategy.** Jump-shift your strategy and strategic process ahead of the point of inflection. Agree on a new overarching strategy, strategic priorities, and cultural changes.

3. **Organization.** Jump-shift your organization and organizational process. Create a new organizational structure and future capability plan in line with your new strategy. Do an immediate role sort. Accelerate individual transitions as appropriate.

4. **Operations.** Jump-shift your operations and operational process, implementing a new approach, flow and management cadence to track and manage your new priorities quarterly, new programs monthly and new projects weekly as appropriate.

5. **Learning and Communication.** Deploy new learning and communication effort in line with your new operating flow and management cadence. This is an ongoing effort, not a one-off event. At every stage of this, every single person in your organization and eco-system will have one question that has to be answered before they can pay attention to anything else: "What does this mean for me?"

Module 2: Stewardship

A big "ah-ha" moment for a number of CEOs is understanding what type of board they need and have. Some without boards realize that having an advisory board can help. Some realize that their boards are controlled by others, operating in the shadows.

Poorly functioning boards often have poorly aligned board members. This can happen when different PE firms are focused on different timelines, or when individual board members get confused about their roles, perhaps having a hard time shifting from being CEO themselves to directing and advising someone else as CEO.

Two keys to working well with any stakeholders are understanding their real motivations and treating them like volunteers.

Board Management Framework

Board Roles:
- Accountable for governance and oversight (noses in.)
- Approve strategic, annual operating (P&L, cash flows, balance sheet), future capability, succession, contingency, and compensation plans.
- Advise on everything else (hands out.)

CEO Role:
- Accountable for strategic, operating, organization plans/results, culture.

Board Management:
Lead Director/Chair accountable for ("owns") board management
- Operations (committees) & board organization.

CEO responsible for board management ("does the work")
- Prepare/brief in advance, manage meetings, follow-up.
- Manage board, group, one-on-one, board two-step (Step 1: Test or consult. Step 2: Sell.)

Module 3: People

Experienced leaders' #1 regret is not moving fast enough on people. Many boot camp attendees commit to investing more in the differential capabilities, freeing up resources by simplifying or outsourcing areas in which they can be merely good enough to invest in those very few areas in which they need to be best-in-class.

Question #1 seems to be where to play. CEOs quickly move on to the importance of culture and the need to build personal relationships with key people – including rising stars and people that can tell them the truth.

<u>BRAVE People Leadership Framework</u>

Environment - Where to play? (Context for people)
Future capability planning in line with overall strategy

Values - What matters and why? (Purpose)
In line with overall mission, vision, guiding principles

Attitudes - How to win? (People choices)
Competitive advantage across acquire, develop, encourage

Relationships - How to connect? (Communication)
Compliance – Contribution – Commitment
(indirect)   (direct)   (emotional)

Behaviors - What impact? (Implementation)
Manage ADEPT talent:
Acquire, Develop, Encourage, Plan and Transition

	<u>Ineffective</u>	<u>Effective</u>	<u>Outstanding</u>
Right Role:	Invest	Support	Cherish
Wrong Role:	Move out	Move laterally	Move up

Module 4: Setting the Stage for BRAVE Innovation

CEOs' main issue with regard to innovation is the conflict between trying to deliver near-term results while paving the way to long-term success. Almost by definition, investment in innovation has a net short-term cost. Some CEOs ask people to innovate (and resource innovation) within their normal jobs. Some set up separate groups. Some accept that they're going to have to fast-follow or acquire other organizations innovating. There is no one right answer.

Environment - Where to play? (Context for innovation)
> The introduction of something new and useful
> Revolutionary/disruptive versus evolutionary/incremental and sustaining

Values - What matters and why? (Purpose of innovation)
> In line with overall mission, vision, guiding principles

Attitudes - How to win? (Innovation choices)
> Products, processes, services, technologies and business model

Relationships - How to connect? (Innovation communication)
> "Unleash the talents and passions of the many from the stranglehold of the few" – Co-create

Behaviors - What impact? (Implementing innovation)
> **CREATE** *(Creative abrasion/collaborative problem solving)* – leverage diverse strengths
> **ITERATE** *(Creative agility/discovery-driven learning)* – "Current Best Thinking"
> **ASSESS** *(Creative resolution/integrated decision-making)* – drowning ugly ducklings
> **IMPLEMENT & SCALE**

Framework for discussion: How best to lead innovation:
1. Acquisitions (like Ebay acquiring PayPal)
2. Sister companies (like Amazon keeping Zappos in the family but separate)
3. Separate divisions (like Disney's Imagineering or Procter & Gamble's Miami Valley Labs)
4. Skunk works (like Lockheed's Skunk Works)
5. Giving all protected time to innovate (like 3M and Google do)
6. Special circumstances (like Hack-a-thons at Facebook, etc.)

Module 5: Communication

CEOs get that inspiring is about communication. It's "Be. Do. Say.". If what you say doesn't match what you do, no one will believe you. If both don't match your fundamental, underlying beliefs, eventually they won't match each other. So, start with who you **be**. Then **do** things in line with those beliefs. Then, you deserve to **say** the words. Be. Do. Say.

BRAVE Communication Framework

Environment - Where to play? (Context)
> Target audience: Internal? External? Contributors, watchers, detractors, (and deciders, influencers, implementers, those in the shadows) – those who care most

Values - What matters and why? (Purpose)
> To you, to the organization, to your audience

Attitudes - How to win? (Choices)
> Platform for change, vision, call to action – headline/mantra/overarching guiding principle, communication points/master narrative

Relationships - How to connect? (Communication)
> Ethos (intentions, competence, empathy), Pathos (feelings), Logos (evidence) => action

Behaviors - What impact? (Implementation)
> MAP: Message + Amplifiers (allies, media) + Persevere (Iterative, ongoing community-building listening and conversations)

You

The CEO Boot Camps and this book are not about specific tactical skills. They're not really "how to" experiences. They're not mid-level management experiences. They are geared to the top of the house.

The magic of a boot camp is in the interactions between CEOs and outside experts as a small group. You won't get that interaction in this book. But you will get a flavor for it to prompt your thinking until you can attend a boot camp or another boot camp live.

Until then I hope this book inspires and enables you to be a BRAVE leader yourself – courageous and deliberate in your behaviors, relationships, attitudes, values and environment at the same time.

Leadership is about inspiring and enabling others to do their absolute best together to realize a meaningful and rewarding shared purpose.

Own the purpose, the vision, the values. Be the chief inspirer.

Delegate almost everything else, focusing on enabling, linking and integrating.

Boot Camp Questions for you to consider:

Scaling up through a point of inflection
- Where to play: What has changed in your situation?
- What matters and why: Changes in your ambition?
- How to win: Your over-arching strategy and strategic resource priorities?
- How win: Changes in your culture?
- How are you going to evolve your culture?
- How connect: What's the right organization and people?
- What impact: What must you do and how must you lead differently?

Stewardship
- What type of board do you have?
- How should you evolve your board – members, structure, processes?
- What works best in influencing your board?
- What must you do to meet the needs of your other stakeholders?

People
- What's your approach to future capability planning?
- What are the three most important behaviors in your organization?
- How are you going to win organizationally? (Acquire, develop, encourage)
- What level of compliance, contribution or commitment are you prompting and rewarding or punishing?
- What people moves should you make faster?

Innovation
- How do you change the context to encourage more innovation?
- What can you do to mash up people with different types of creativity?
- How do you improve your innovation process?

Communication
- Who cares most?
- What matters and why to those who care most?
- What are the core elements of your narrative? (Mantra, idea, guiding principle, message points)
- What's the ethos, pathos and logos (me, you, us) of your own story?
- Who and what helps you amplify your story over time?
- Who's controlling your online presence?
- How prepared is your organization to react to a crisis?

Module 1: Scaling up through a point of inflection

Deming told us, "Every system is perfectly designed to produce the results it gets." Then Intel's Andy Grove defined a point of inflection as, "An event that changes the way we think and act."

When that event, that a change in your situation or ambition occurs, change your system to change your results. Change your strategy, organization, and operations together, simultaneously, in sync, to avoid breaking the system as you scale through a point of inflection.

The BRAVE Leadership framework outlines a set of questions to guide your thinking and process from the outside in.

Environment	Where to play?	(Context)
Values	What matters and why?	(Purpose)
Attitudes	How to win?	(Choices)
Relationships	How to connect?	(Communication)
Behaviors	What impact?	(Implementation)

Environment. First, interpret and create context for your team. Understand your organization's history (including founder's legacy), recent results, and changes in the business and competitive environment to guide *where to play*. If you're happy with your current trajectory, you can scale gradually over time. If there's more urgency, you'll want to scale ahead of the need.

Ferdinand de Lesseps successfully led the building of the Suez Canal and was then convicted and sentenced to prison for his failed attempt to build a similar canal in Panama. His successful approach to the flat, dry Suez desert was doomed from the start in the hilly, rainy, disease-ridden jungle of Panama. Environment or context is not the sole determinant of success or failure, but it must inform your attitude and approach.

Flush with his success in Suez, de Lesseps drove a "congress" of scientists, engineers and others to back his choice of Panama for a canal and a sea level approach to avoid the use of locks. His super-human confidence enabled him to assemble the political, financial and human resources required to tackle the project. But that same confidence blinded him to others' points of view resulting in 800,000 backers losing all their investment and 20,000 workers losing their lives to tropical diseases before the project was abandoned.

Be clear on the difference between cyclical and systematic changes. The seasons rotate through spring, summer, autumn and fall each year. But the increased fire season in places like California is a systemic change. Don't believe me? Just go as PG&E, the local utility

Netflix saw the change from bricks and mortar to direct mail and made Blockbuster obsolete. Then they saw the coming change to streaming and made their own direct mail business obsolete (with a short misstep with Quickster.) Then they moved into content. Net (pun intended,) they are keeping the cannibals in the family.

???

Boot Camp question for you to consider:

Where to play: What has changed in your situation?

???

Values. Mission, vision and values are the foundation of your culture, your organization, and your future. Clarify *what matters and why* - the good you and your team do and the guiding principles you choose to follow. Align all around any changes in your purpose and ambitions.

Kate Farms' Richard and Michelle Laver[1] provide an example of how people don't get to choose their missions. Their mission found them as dealing with their daughter's disease required them to invent a new way for her to get nutrition. This is what Simon Sinek calls a compelling why.

---

[1] Adapted from my November 26, 2013 Forbes.com article, *Why You Don't Get To Choose Your Mission. It Chooses You*

Mission is not a choice. It's dictated by others' needs. Sometimes those others give you a mission. Sometimes you have to figure it out yourself. Either way, it's a journey of discovery, not creation.

The questions to ask are:

- Who needs us?
- What do they need and why?
- What must we deliver to meet their needs?

Your mission flows from those. This is true whether you are onboarding into a new leadership role or just re-thinking what matters and why.

Richard and Michelle Laver's story about the -daughter Kate was born with Cerebral Palsy, which made eating normal food out of the question. As Richard explained to me,

> *At the age of four, Kate was failing to 'thrive' and was faced with numerous difficulties. The meal replacement shake her doctors prescribed was overloaded with sugar and dairy for calorie enhancement…We were in the hospital with Kate in dire circumstances — she could not keep any weight on her and her quality of life was poor. Getting Kate out of that was our driving force.*

Enough was enough.

> *Michelle and I decided it was time to take matters into our own hands to try and alleviate Kate's symptoms and together we tried to find the most holistic ingredients we could so that our daughter would start feeling better.*

So, with the help of an industry expert they blended 21 super foods including but not limited to acai, mangosteen, raspberries, black currants, green tea extract, etc., with antioxidants, high protein and vitamin rich ingredients and put together the world's first dairy-free, gluten-free and soy-free ready-to-drink meal replacement shake. It worked. Richard went on to relate that Kate *"has never been to the hospital again. Within weeks of drinking Komplete, Kate's condition improved greatly and she no longer needed breathing treatment for sleep apnea, her digestion problems were a thing of the past and her mouth was once again healthy."*

Many people build businesses by developing systematic ways to solve a problem shared by many others. That's exactly what Richard and Michelle did, assembling resources and then building distribution step-by-step to build a business. But at every step of the way, they've kept a picture of Kate front and center – in the company's name, on their website, in their minds and hearts.

Implications for You

Let Kate find you. Your Kate may personify a disease, an injustice, an inconvenience, or any other problem in search of a solution. Whatever it is, make sure it matters to you and to the people you're going to bring to bear to develop and eventually market that solution.

Those of you trying to pull everyone together to co-create an inspiring mission for your organization are going about the task exactly backwards. You don't get to create your mission. It already exists. Just be open to the call when it finds you.

The Madison County Indiana high school football Cubs had 3 wins, 27 losses in three years under their previous coach. Want to guess what new coach, Patric Morrison saw as his mission?

As the Indy Star reported, "It had nothing to do with football, and everything to do with wanting to save kids from a darkness engulfing a county with a 2016 suicide rate three times higher than the national average. All he wanted was to create a place where the kids felt safe.

Imagine you are a brain surgeon. Imagine you invent a procedure that can reduce the mortality of a certain type of brain surgery from 30% to zero. What's the one thing you should never do again? Operate. Your ambition should change from saving lives (yourself) to teaching others to save lives. Any moment you spend operating is a missed opportunity to scale by teaching others.

Values

People actually follow visions and values when they commit to them, see them turned into followable guiding principles, practice them consistently and have them reinforced.[2] We've become so used to people's actions having so little in common with organizations' stated values that it's hardly even noteworthy when that happens. If job No. 1 for any CEO is to own the vision and values, they fail if people aren't following them. These four steps can make that happen.

1) Commit to values

If you want your people to commit to your vision and values you need to let them co-create them. You're going to get the commitment you deserve. Tell and you'll get compliance. Invite contribution and you'll get contribution. Commitment requires real co-creation. If you can't do that, stop reading here and put tight controls in place because your people are going to do what they think they can away with.

2) Turn your values into followable guiding principles

Bill Belicheck has this right. Recruit for values. Manage with guiding principles. Values are important. But they are ethereal. People may know they're good. But they don't know what to do with them. Guiding principles tell them what to do without the constraint of policies.

People happily work in an organization that values the team. They know what to do in an organization that guides them to commit to support and collaborate with each other. The closer you get to one over-arching guiding principle, the easier it is to follow.

---

[2] From my April 24, 2018 Forbes.com article, *How to Get People to Actually Follow Your Vision and Values*

3) Practice those value-based guiding principles consistently

"We are what we repeatedly do. Excellence, then, is not an act, but a habit." – Will Durant. Commitment gives you desire. Guidelines give you direction. Practice makes it stick.

Embed your values through guiding principles brought to life in your ADEPT talent practices (Acquire, Develop, Encourage, Plan, Transition.)

Identify and recruit people who share your values and bring them onboard in a way that reflects your value-based guiding principles.

Develop people in line with your guiding principles.

Recognize and reward people in line with your guiding principles. The results they deliver matter. The way they deliver those results matters just as much.

Take your guiding principles into account as you plan and transition people across, up or out.

Everything communicates. People will notice if these efforts follow or do not follow your guiding principles.

4) Reinforce your vision and values over and over again

As the CEO, owner, leader, you must own the vision and values. And you must own them all the time.

Atrium Health's President and CEO Gene Woods drives their mission "to improve health, elevate hope and advance healing, for all" all the time. He starts *every* meeting with what is known throughout the organization as a "Connect to Purpose." Every meeting. Every board meeting. Every leadership meeting. In fact, every gathering within in the organization begins in this same way. Different teammates and even invited guests are encouraged to highlight stories to remind themselves about what matters and remain connected to the positive impact they make.

You can see this in their <u>annual report</u>. It's full of stories like "Who is Madie DeBruhl?" (12-year-old bone marrow transplant patient.) Or "Who is Shelly Cooley?" (Nurse who goes well beyond the call of duty to help other people grow.) Or "Who is Lee Beatty?" (Family medicine physician who epitomizes how to "Deliver the gift of humanity.")

Over the past couple of years, I've worked with two companies where safety was paramount in the heavy manufacturing and coal mining space. Each of those companies started every meeting with a "Safety minute." Someone in the meeting had to share an idea or provide an update that would help everyone in the meeting be safe.

When I ran the Puritan cooking oil business, we were all about "healthy." I started every meeting by asking how that meeting was either going to make our consumers healthier or our business healthier. If people didn't know the answer, I walked out. People learned what they had to do to get me to stay.

If you choose to have a values-driven organization, the end does not justify the means.[3] For these organizations, guiding principles are the bedrock upon which they build their culture. These are things they will not sacrifice even if it means their mission will fail. Hence the question, what matters and why.

Values may be words like these:

- Company 1: Communication, Respect, Integrity, Excellence.
- Company 2: Social Responsibility, Sustainability, Partnership, Volunteering.

Hard to argue with these words. Unfortunately, company 1 was Enron. Company 2 was Volkswagen. Neither of these companies' leadership acted in line with their values. And that was their undoing. Enron is gone, leaving behind a trail of pain in its wake. Volkswagen's faked emission-testing results have severely its brand.

---

[3] From my January 24, 2018 Forbes.com article, *The Second Question for BRAVE Leaders: What Matters and Why?*

Conversely, Procter & Gamble bought Norwich Eaton, and dropped Charlie Carroll in as general manager. When Charlie visited the Norwich operation in Mexico, he was presented with Norwich Mexico's leading drug – the number one selling drug in all of Mexico.

"What does it do?"

"It's a placebo. In your country doctors say 'take two aspirin and call me in the morning'. Here doctors have people take two of these. It works half the time. And because it's a placebo, it has absolutely no side effects. Anyone can take it."

"Pull it off the market immediately."

Charlie didn't hesitate. Charlie didn't have to call anyone at headquarters to clear his decision. He knew that selling a placebo violated Procter & Gamble's guiding principle of doing the right thing.

At one point another Procter & Gamble employee had presented P&G's VP of advertising, Richard Goldstein with what he thought was a tough choice. Richard didn't see it that way at all.

"Let's do this."

"But that will cost us business."

"Principles are only principles when they hurt."

This is the difference between hollow words on a wall and principles that actually guide choices.

For example, one organization had three core values: caring, doing and delivering. One of their region teams took those fine values and turned them into something to guide their actions with and through customers to end users. They got to these:

Caring:

1. **Own the Impact.** Be zealous and contagiously confident in the positive impact we make on [end users] together through the lens of the customer.

Doing:

2. **Be the Elite** (personally and professionally) – Be the best possible subject-matter experts to partner with: We listen, understand, and help.

3. **Blaze the Trail**. We live and breathe ever-better products, service and relationships contributing to each other's' and our customers' success.

Delivering:

4. **Get It Done**. We get it done better, faster, and more efficiently - close the closeable through customized solutions for our customer.

There's a lot good about these. They nest within the company's overall values. They are action-oriented and personal. And they guide choices.

Implications for you

If your people are living by the right values, this is a low priority exercise for you. If enough of your people are not doing the right the things, think about asking people to lay out a set of guiding principles that flow from your values.

Note you're going to get the employee engagement you deserve.

- If you write the guiding principles yourself, you can certainly force compliance.
- If you want your people to contribute their best efforts, you have to invite them to contribute to the guiding principles.
- If you want your people to commit to the cause and your guiding principles you need to let them co-create them. If just the senior leadership team co-creates the guiding principles, they will commit. If all your management co-

creates the guiding principles, that broader group will commit. If you want everyone to commit, everyone needs to be part of the co-creation. This is the least efficient and messiest way to do this, and the only way to deserve broad-based commitment. Your choice.

???

Boot Camp question for you to consider:

What matters and why? Changes in your ambition?

???

Attitude is the Pivot Point

As you work to evolve your culture, focus on attitudes. There's a strong case to be made that IBM's near-death experience was a result of a bad attitude. It thought it was the best. It thought its customers needed it more than it needed its customers. It stopped being flexible. The big thing Lou Gerstner did was reversing that attitude. Behaviors and relationships followed.

More recently, we've seen the same thing at Hewlett-Packard. It started believing its own myths and lost the congruence between strategy and posture. Meg Whitman could be successful only if she was able to change the organization's attitude.

Of course, I am oversimplifying things. Few things are as simple as we hope they are. Of course, you have to be in touch with your environment. Of course, you have to make sure your values are current. Of course, people and communication matter. Of course, it's all theoretical gibberish until someone actually does something that impacts someone else. Attitude is not the only lever. But it's generally the lever to pull first, using that choice or change to influence the others.

Pivot around strategy, priorities and culture choices. Start with choices around your overarching strategy and priorities across the value chain and then be sure they sync with your culture to scale *how to win*. The most effective organizations have one single overarching strategy which guides their resource allocation priorities so people are clear where they need to be best-in-class, world class, strong, or merely cost-effectively good enough to create value.[4]

Strategic Alignment:

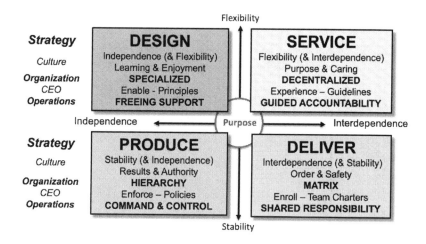

GE has failed the cocktail napkin test. If you can't explain your strategy to someone on the back of a cocktail napkin, it's too complicated. The best-performing organizations have a single, overarching strategy that everyone in the organization understands. More complicated organizations end up tripping over themselves. That's why GE is going to split up. Many of its individual businesses are focused. The conglomerate as a whole is not.

Strategic planning is about generating and selecting broad options to deal with barriers and close gaps between current realities and objectives. A good strategy guides the creation and allocation of resources to the right place, in the right way, at the right time, over time to bring to fruition your mission, vision, objectives and goals while following guiding principles.

---

[4] Adapted from my January 17, 2018 Forbes.com article, *GE's Impending Breakup's Underlying Root Cause: The Need For A Single Overarching Strategy*

A slight update to Porter's model suggests organizations should pick one point on the value chain at which to focus in addition to the selling that everyone must do: invention, production, delivery, and experience. Your single overarching strategy should identify the right way to build and leverage unique strengths relative to competitors at your choice of one of those points.

Strategic priorities flow from that single overarching strategy and guide choices across the other points on the value chain by clarifying in which you need to be "Best-in-class'/superior (top 10%), "World class"/parity with the best (top 25%), "Strong"/above average or "Good enough." In general, you'll want to invest in the first two and simplify, scale or outsource the last.

Take four examples in fashion/retail. Gucci is best in class in design, Zara in production, Amazon in distribution, and bridal boutiques in service or guest experience.

GE's lack of focus

GE plays across the entire value chain: Invent – produce – deliver – experience.

- GE invents. They "develop the next generation large additive machines."
- GE produces as a "world-leading manufacturer for jet engines."
- GE delivers, combining "decades of industrial leadership with cutting-edge data science and analytics acumen to create an efficient, productive and reliable digital-rail ecosystem."
- GE provides a complete experience, supporting its customers with its "leasing, financing, services and consulting."

It is not possible to do this as a unified company. The different points in the value chain require completely different cultures.

- **Inventing** the next generation of large additive machines requires an innovation-centered culture in which people are encouraged to take risks and rewarded for taking those risks whether they result in the next revolutionary step or helpful learning.
- **Producing** world-leading jet engines requires a disciplined culture in which people are rewarded for consistency and reliability. When jet engines fail, lives are at risk.
- **Delivering** across an efficient, productive and reliable digital-rail ecosystem requires a culture of systems thinkers orchestrating multiple parts and players as a cohesive whole.
- Providing an **experience** across leasing, financing, services and consulting requires a culture of service. People working here must think customer-first and pull existing solutions together in response to customers' needs.

There's much to be learned from Thomas Edison as an inventor and from Jack Welch as the ultimate creator of value in a conglomerate. Now, the leveling influence of the Internet has meant that winning organizations will be the ones with single overarching strategic postures, supported by clear strategic priorities completely aligned with their cultures.

Basics for you

- **Strategy**: The overarching strategy guiding all choices.
- **Priorities:** Resource choices in line with that strategy.
- **Culture:** Behaviors, relationships, attitudes, values, environment.

Push yourself and your leaders to get to one overarching strategy — simple enough to explain on a cocktail napkin. That strategy should make clear where you play and your core competitive advantage.

Be brutal about choices in the strategic priorities required to deliver that overarching strategy, investing in the very few things in which you must be either best-in-class or world class and decisively simplifying, scaling or outsourcing the things that need be only good enough.

Make sure your cultural behaviors, relationships, attitudes, values and environment are aligned with that overarching strategy and priorities. Just like GE, your strategies will evolve over time. Your people will change. In the end, the only sustainable competitive advantage is your organization's culture.

Apple, Coca-Cola, Wal-Mart, Ritz-Carlton, have distinctive attitudes, focusing their strategies, priorities, and culture on a) independent design/invention, b) stable, consistent production, c) interdependent delivery, and d) flexible customer-experience-focused service respectively.

Once you pick your one single over-arching strategy (design, produce, deliver or experience,) you need to determine your resource priorities so all are clear in which areas you choose to be:

- Best-in-class - superiority (top 10%)
- World class – parity (top quartile)
- Strong – above average
- Good enough.

??

Boot Camp question for you to consider:

How to win? Your over-arching strategy and strategic resource priorities?

??

Culture

Given enough time and money, your competitors can duplicate almost everything you've got working for you.[5] They can hire away some of your best people. They can reverse engineer your processes. The only thing they can't duplicate is your culture.

Hire Away the Best People

Guy bumps into a competitor's star engineer at a trade event:

"Would you come work for us if we gave you $1 million/year?"

"I would."

"How about $50,000/year?"

"What do you think I am?

"We've already established that. Now we're negotiating."

While not everyone is for sale, enough are to make you vulnerable.

Reverse Engineer Processes

Even if you've got things patented, trademarked or cloaked in multiple layers of secrecy, your competitors can see what you deliver, what you get done and the core pieces of how you do it. Even if they can't duplicate what you do exactly, they can get close enough to hurt you - or take it to the next level and render your processes obsolete.

Brave Cultures Are Sustainable

All music is made from the same 12 notes. All culture is made from the same five components: behaviors, relationships, attitudes, values and environment. It's the way those notes or components are put together that makes things sing.

---

[5] Adapted from my February 8, 2012 Forbes.com article, *Corporate Culture: The Only Truly Sustainable Competitive Advantage*

In sustainable, championship cultures, behaviors (the way we do things here) are inextricably linked to relationships, informed by attitudes, built on a rock-solid base of values, and completely appropriate for the environment in which the organization chooses to operate.

As Simon Sinek famously pointed out, most organizations think what – how – why. Great leaders and great organizations start with why (environment and values), then look at how (attitudes and relationships) before getting to what (behaviors).

- Behaviors: What impact? *Implementation.*
- Relationships: How to connect? *Communication.*
- Attitude: How to win? *Choices.*
- Values: What matters and why? *Purpose.*
- Environment: Where to play? *Context.*

It's the context that makes it so hard to duplicate a championship culture. Because every organization's environment is different, matching someone else's behaviors, relationships, attitudes, and values will not produce the same culture.

???

Boot Camp question for you to consider:

How win? Changes in your culture?

???

Changing culture

Jeff Leitner is a mentor with a particular set of skills. He has an ability to identify the hidden forces, unwritten rules and underlying beliefs that are socially reinforced to keep things from changing. And he has developed ways to change things as part of solving tough societal problems.

He explained to me that

1. Most change fails (as in 70-80% of changes) - because of culture.
2. The key is identifying the hidden forces, unwritten rules, and underlying beliefs that are socially reinforced to keep change from happening.
3. There are four ways to deal with these change blockers: the wrong way, the easy way, the intermediate way, and the advanced way.

The wrong way to deal with these change blockers is to write new rules. Won't work. You'll get passive-aggressive resistance all over the place.

Coca-Cola Japan's leadership team was at an annual planning meeting in Atlanta. Our largest and most profitable brand in Japan was Georgia Coffee. For perspective, this was 1995 and at that point the Coca-Cola system made over $1 Billion in profit on this brand in Japan. It was sold only in Japan. (That's going to become important in a moment.)

We agreed to change Georgia's brand positioning. The "we" included Doug Ivester, Coca-Cola's CEO, Sergio Zyman, Coca-Cola's Chief Marketing Officer and the senior leadership team of Coca-Cola Japan.

When we got back to Japan, I informed the Georgia team of the positioning change.

Several weeks later, I was going out to make a presentation to one of Coca-Cola's bottlers. People prepared slides for me in Japanese – which I could not read – and I presented them in English with simultaneous translations.

When I checked the Georgia positioning slide, I noticed it hadn't changed and called out the mistake to Georgia's brand leader.

"I think you gave me the wrong positioning for Georgia."

"No Bradt-san. It's right."

"It can't be right. Here's the slide I used six months ago. It's identical to this slide. But I know the positioning changed when we were in Atlanta last month."

"Oh Bradt-san, only the Atlanta positioning changed. The local, Japanese positioning did not change."

Do you get it? The brand was only sold in Japan. The Atlanta positioning was a complete myth and had no bearing on what happened in any market in the world. The only positioning that mattered was the local Japanese positioning which was completely hidden from senior management.

The new, written rules were completely irrelevant.

The easy way to deal with unwritten rules is to walk away. Accept that you can't change them or solve the problem and go play somewhere else.

Witness how the British navy got people to start eating citrus fruits by putting them on ships and saying they were for officer only.

The intermediate way is to find deviant ways to go around the rules, distracting the keepers of the unwritten rules with other changes.

Your team needs disrupters, rebels, challengers, and deviants to help it evolve and survive. Deviant behavior can subvert the social norms - informal, unspoken rules - preventing you from solving problems.[6]

1. Every tough problem is held in place by one or more problematic social norms.
2. See the actors, history, limits, future, configuration, and parthood, then think about norms and deviance, before deviating from the norm to solve the problem.

---

[6] From my November 6, 2018 Forbes.com article, *In Praise of Deviants*

Some definitions:

- **Actors** are the people involved in problems – directly, influencing or not.
- **History** is the stories people tell – true, false or nonsense.
- **Limits** are explicit rules and laws that influence how people behave.
- **Future** is the set of beliefs people have about what is likely, possible or impossible.
- **Configuration** is labels or categories people use – whether or not they actually make sense.
- **Parthood** is how your problems relate to other problems through shared actors, settings, or resources.
- **Norms** are the informal, unspoken rules that really explain what's going on.
- **Deviance** is an existing or new behavior outside the norms.

Deviance can be positive or negative, evolutionary or revolutionary, unintentional or deliberate.

Positive deviations move you in desired directions where negative deviations do the opposite. Evolutionary deviations are incremental, where revolutionary deviations are major step changes. Unintentional deviations happen without foresight or planning as opposed to planned, deliberate deviations. You want positive deviations whether they are evolutionary, revolutionary, unintentional or deliberate.

How to get more positive deviance

Note the ABCs of behavior modification: Antecedents, Behaviors, Consequences. People do things because antecedents prompt them. They do them again because of the balance of consequences: rewarding or punishing desirable or undesirable behavior.

To get more positive deviation, start by prompting it. Hire for differential strengths to get people on your team who can do different things better than can your existing team members. Hire for differential preferences to nudge your culture in a new direction. Then explicitly invite people to challenge existing norms.

It's all for naught if you don't change the balance of consequences as well.

Imagine I'm standing next to you and ask you to shake my hand. You do. I look you in the eye, smile, and say thank you. If I then ask you to shake my hand again, you likely will.

You shook my hand both times because I asked you. You shook my hand the second time partly because the consequences of the first handshake were positive – assuming you appreciated my smile and "thank you." On the other hand (pun intended,) if instead of looking you in the eye, smiling and saying thank you, I take your hand and then punch you in the face with my other hand, you will be less inclined to shake my hand again.

If you want positive change, you must dial up the positive consequences and dial down the negative consequences of desired behaviors, and do the opposite for undesired behavior. Stop punching people in the face for doing things you want them to do – especially when it comes to positive changes that violate existing norms. And make sure others don't punish your deviants for doing things differently.

Boss comes by subordinate's desk holding a memo. "Did I ask you to write this?" "No." Boss puts the memo in the subordinate's trash bin, effectively punching him in the face for thinking on his own.

Too many people get shunned for working harder or smarter or going an extra mile for an internal or external customer by others thinking they are being made to look bad or feeling threatened in some way. Be explicit about the need for deviance and apply the ABCs to behaviors supporting or hindering that deviance as well as to the deviance itself.

The advanced way to influence change is to turn the unwritten rules on their head, changing them from blocking change to assisting change. Leitner has a series of questions he uses to get at this:

ACTORS

What people or groups are directly involved in your problem? (1st order)

Who influences the people or groups directly involved in your problem? (2nd order)

Who plays an important role by not being around?

What are the motivations or interests of people directly involved in your problem?

HISTORY

How do people say your problem started?

How do people explain why your problem is still around?

What would people say are the most important events in your problem's story?

What falsehoods do people spread about your problem?

(Look at true, false, half-truth and nonsense stories.)

LIMITS

What are some of the rules and laws that influence how people behave around your problem?

Which rules related to your problem do people usually follow and which ones do they usually ignore?

How do people respond to limits of time and money related to your problem?

What laws of nature are specifically related to your problem?

(follow, break, ignore, change)

FUTURE

What is the most common belief about the future of your problem?

What do people believe is possible, but unlikely to happen with your problem?

What single event might people say would change the future of your problem?

What do people believe could never, ever happen in the future of your problem?

CONFIGURATION

What official labels or categories do people use when talking about your problem?

What informal labels or categories do people use when talking about your problem?

What labels or categories might you use when describing your problem to an outsider? (make or do not make sense)

PARTHOOD

What problems are obviously related to your problem?

What other problems would outsiders be surprised are related to your problem?

What other problems do actors in your problem worry about?

What other problems would disappear if your problem were resolved?

(all connected somehow - shared actors, settings, resources)

NORMS

Now take the clues you found by answering questions on the previous six pages and piece them together to find some previously invisible social norms.

What are the social situations you most associate with your problem?

What do actors do in relation to your problem that can't be explained by laws or formal, explicit rules?

Somebody keeps actors related to your problem in line. Who is it?

Now that you understand the whole process, here's a bonus question:

Which of the norms you unearthed is problematic and keeping your problem unsolved?

DEVIANCE

Finally, think about a behavior so powerful that it could subvert the problematic, unhealthy norm you identified.

Is there an existing behavior out there that could ultimately change the norms related to your problem?

Can you imagine a new behavior that could ultimately change the norms related to your problem?

???

Boot Camp question for you to consider:

How are you going to evolve your culture?

???

Relationships. Everything you do, say, listen to, observe communicates - 24/7/365, forever. This is the heart of leadership - inspiring and enabling others to comply, contribute or commit. Let strategy drive structure and *how to connect,* moving from purpose and message to stories to narrative tying the stories together to create meaning, alignment and accelerated results.

WNET's Neal Shapiro[7], provides a good example of leveraging a single, simplifying message of "innovation and re-invention" in ongoing iterative conversations.

> *Every time we were beginning to form up into teams, we would be reorganized. I was to learn later in life that we tend to meet new situations by reorganizing...and a wonderful method it can be for creating the illusion of progress while producing confusion, inefficiency, and demoralization.* - Attributed to Petronius Arbiter, d. A.D. 65, Roman governor and advisor (arbiter) to Nero

Reorganizing your people or your ideas is seductive, giving you "the illusion of progress". Don't get me wrong. We're all new leaders all the time. And sometimes reorganizing is exactly the right thing to do. But often, sticking with the same thing for a while gives you and your team the chance to build momentum. Neal Shapiro gives us a good example of that during his tenure as CEO of WNET.

From his very first day in January, 2008, Shapiro has been driving a message of innovation and re-invention. As he puts it,

> *It's the only way to stay relevant; it's the only way to stay in business...and that has had its challenges since many people have worked here for more than 20 years.*

Shapiro's first effort to communicate his message was to create new programs centered around WNET's core strength of arts and culture: two weekly local arts programs--one called Sunday Arts, which features the great museum exhibits, films, galleries and performances going on in New York City, and the other called Reel 13, which airs on Saturday nights and pairs a classic movie with an indie film and a short film created by our viewers. WNET had not truly taken advantage of creating programming to reflect the rich cultural offerings in the city—nor the artistic talent of its viewers.

---

[7] Adapted from my August 24, 2011 Forbes.com article, *The Power of a Consistent Message Illustrated by WNET's CEO, Neal Shapiro*

Other ways he drove his message of innovation and reinvention included:

- Tapping into the trend of **user generated content** and launched a documentary in which viewers sent in video and interviews.
- Taking down the existing website, which had limited video, and replacing it with a **content rich, video centric site** that PBS used as a model to create its own web video player;
- Launching an international news program called World Focus, where Shapiro encouraged **laptop editing**, which saved considerable amounts of money, and more efficient use of partnerships (Associated Press, Al Jazeera and others) to cut down on field reporting expenses;
- Building a two-story studio within Lincoln Center with **cost-efficient robotic cameras** and a set which can be used for many different purposes.

The impact has been meaningful. In March of this year, in response to an RFP from the Governor of New Jersey, Shapiro spearheaded WNET's proposal to take over NJN, the New Jersey state-run television network. Last month, their proposal was accepted and on July 1st, they debuted "NJTV"—their rename of the network—to the citizens of New Jersey.

There have been many changes at WNET during the past 3 years—but Shapiro's core message has remained the same: innovate, reinvent, or go out of business.

The point is not that leaders should say the same thing over and over again. The point is that consistency of core message over time has a multiplier effect. Shapiro brought his message to life with what he did and what he encouraged others to do.

Everything communicates. You can either make choices in advance about what and how you're going to communicate or react to what others do. It is important to discover your own message and be clear on your platform for change, vision, and call to action before you start trying to inspire others. It will evolve as you learn, but you can't lead unless you have a starting point to help focus those learning plans. Identify your target audiences. Craft and leverage your core message and master narrative. Monitor and adjust as appropriate on an ongoing basis.

The strategy change to scale up at a point of inflection dictates a new set of required capabilities. Do a new future capability plan and then start bridging the gaps between your current and the required organization aligned with your core strategy: likely specialized for design, a hierarchy for producing, a matrix for delivery, decentralized for service.

???

Boot Camp question for you to consider:

How connect? What's the right organization and people?

???

Behaviors. It's all theoretical gibberish until put it into actions that result in impact and effect. Re-think your operations to provide freeing support, command and control, shared responsibility, or guided accountability as appropriate. This is the third leg of your system. If you change strategy and organization without changing the way you and your team work, things fall down.

Like P&G's John Pepper[8] whose actions consistently matched his words and fundamental beliefs, you lead with your feet and actions, more than with what you say.

Voting with his feet to encourage a young brand manager

I was a young brand manager showing up for work on a typical day. I got into the elevator to go to my office on the 4th floor. Mr. Pepper got in to go to the 11th floor – where the big dogs sat. At the time he

---

[8] Adapted from my August 3, 2011 Forbes.com article, *Procter & Gamble's John Pepper Votes With His Feet*

was the EVP of the company's entire U.S. operations. I had never spoken to him alone.

Between the 1st and the 4th floors we exchanged greetings and he asked me what I was working on. Then, to my surprise, he got off the elevator with me on my floor to continue the conversation, voting with his feet to show his support. When we were done several minutes later, he asked me to send him a brief write up, which he then circulated as an example of a good initiative.

It's hard to describe how wonderful that made me feel.

Voting with his feet in support of the organization

A couple of years later, there was a P&G annual managers meeting – 13,000 managers in the Cincinnati Coliseum - just after it had been announced that Ed Artzt was going to be the new CEO and not the man most had expected, John Pepper.

When Artzt entered the meeting to give his talk, he received a nice round of applause. When Pepper came out later, he got a nine-and-a-half-minute standing ovation. Every single person in the crowd wanted him to know how he or she felt.

And then Pepper voted with his feet again by not leaving. Having been passed over for the P&G CEO slot, he could have gone to all sorts of places in an instant. But he didn't. He loved P&G and stayed on in the role the company asked him to fill.

When Artzt's tenure as CEO was over, Pepper got the nod and became one of P&G's most beloved CEOs ever.

Voting with his feet to help a P&G alum

When we started CEO Connection and its CEO Boot Camps in 2005, the first person I called to invite to deliver an opening address was John Pepper. Although he probably didn't remember who I was (the elevator interaction surely had a greater impact on me than on him), he said yes in an instant. It didn't matter who I was. He knew that if I had worked at P&G, I likely shared the same values as he did. And one of those values was supporting fellow alums. (His talk was wonderful by the way).

Implementation. Start with one of four primary strategies: 1) Design, 2) Produce, 3) Deliver, or 4) Service. Let that drive associated cultural, organizational, and operational choices. And let that inform what "CEO" means, as the CEO should be the Chief Enablement, Enforcement, Enrollment or Experience Officer depending upon the core strategic choice.

The world needs three types of leaders[9] influencing feelings (artistic), knowledge (scientific) and actions (interpersonal). As an interpersonal leader, the only way to achieve your vision, in line with your values, in the context you choose, is through the attitude, relationships, and behaviors you model and engender in the people you lead. It's not about you. It's about the cause. It's not enough to have compliant followers, doing what they must. It's not even enough to have contributing followers. You need followers committed to a deserving cause. Be BRAVE yourself and help them be BRAVE individually and together in a winning BRAVE culture.

When people see or hear "leader", they generally think of interpersonal leaders inspiring and enabling teams. While those interpersonal leaders are of critical import, the world needs artistic leaders and scientific leaders just as much. And you need to play your part.

Webster defines leader as "a person who rules, guides, or inspires others".

Artistic leaders inspire by influencing feelings. They help us take new approaches to how we see, hear, taste, smell and touch things. You can find these leaders creating new designs, new art, and the like. These people generally have no interest in ruling or guiding. They are all about changing perceptions.

---

[9] Adapted from my January 29, 2014 Forbes.com article, *The Three Types Of Leaders The World Needs Most: Artistic, Scientific and Interpersonal*

Scientific leaders guide <u>and</u> inspire by influencing knowledge with their thinking and ideas. You can find them creating new technologies, doing research and writing, teaching and the like. Their ideas tend to be well thought-through, supported by data and analysis, and logical. These people develop structure and frameworks that help others solve problems.

Interpersonal leaders can be found ruling, guiding and inspiring at the head of their interpersonal cohort whether it's a team, organization, or political entity. They come in all shapes and sizes, and influence actions in different ways. The common dimension across interpersonal leaders is that they are leading other people.

Net, Artistic leaders inspire by influencing feelings. Scientific leaders guide and inspire by influencing knowledge. Interpersonal leaders rule, guide and inspire to influence actions. And, oh by the way, these are not mutual exclusive. Leaders can lead in more than one way.

A More Sophisticated Approach to People and Personalities

Don Fornes, CEO of Software Advice has taken this to heart. He realizes it is *"worthwhile to think in a sophisticated way about people and personalities."* So, he commissioned a business psychologist, Dr. James Maynard, to analyze the highest-performers at his company to see what makes them so unique. The goal was to better understand his team, learn what makes his people tick, how to better (and more effectively) manage them, and how to identify and hire more people like them.

While there are all sorts of different profiles, Fornes took me through four in particular, Savant, Champ, Matrix Thinker, and Giver. In brief, and hugely oversimplified

Savants are "really good at what they do". But are usually really good at just one thing, like writing, researching, engineering, creating. At their core, they love to learn. Savants may be scientific or artistic leaders but are often introverted.

Champs strive to be the best and to overcome the chips on their shoulders. Look for these outspoken, assertive people to be leading the charge in sales or political campaigns.

Matrix Thinkers are trailblazers and problems solvers. These people can be creative, project-oriented and strong interpersonal leaders.

Givers make great team players. They are loyal and give it their all. These people do particularly well in producer roles, central HQ roles, and customer service roles.

Fornes and his leadership team made this information practical by using it as a guide to inspiring and enabling these people. His managers now work hard not to over-manage Savants, not to overload Matrix Thinkers, to keep up with Champs, and to take care of Givers.

BRAVE Leaders

The BRAVE Leadership framework applies to all leaders. Artistic, scientific and interpersonal leaders should ask the same five BRAVE questions around behaviors, relationships, attitudes, values and the environment. Since they are asking them through different lenses they may ask them differently and get different answers.

	Interpersonal	Scientific	Artistic
Where to play?	Context	Problems	Media
What matter / why?	The Cause	Solutions	Perceptions
How to win?	Rally the team	Better thinking	New approach
How to connect?	Hearts	Minds	Souls
What impact?	Actions	Knowledge	Feelings

Implications for You

Broaden your horizons. Cherish your artistic, scientific and interpersonal leaders. Lead in the way that works best for you whether you are a Giver, Matrix Thinker, Savant, or Champ with a chip on your shoulder. Either way, pay attention to the art and science of team optimization as leading is too important to be left just to the rulers.

Then decide your role. In general, if you've got a design-focused strategy, you probably need to be the chief enabler, getting your designers what they need.

If you've got a production-focused strategy, you should be the chief enforcer, driving discipline and stability.

If you've got a distribution-focused strategy, you should be the chief enroller, bringing in people across the matrix and eco-system to make things work.

If you're a service-focused organization, you should be the chief experience officer, making everyone think customer-first every time, all the time.

The ability to delegate is critical. Focus on working less and creating more value.[10]

Scope is a function of resources and time. If the scope of what you're trying to accomplish is too much to get done in a high quality way, you have to add resources, add time, or cut back the scope. In other words, say "no" to some of the less important items and non-value-adding steps.

[10] Adapted from my November 29, 2012 Forbes.com article, *Work Less, Create More Value – The Art of Delegating*

Think in terms of your options for completing tasks:

1. Do well yourself
2. Do yourself, but just well enough
3. Delegate and supervise
4. Delegate and ignore
5. Do later
6. Do never

Working harder is often counter-productive. As Simpler Consulting CEO Marc Hafer explained to me, the world is full of heroes who get in the way – the *"bright, passionate, compassionate ones who are blinded by their passion."* They strive to *"get it done"* at any cost, not realizing the true cost is the diminished effort against other, higher value adding activities.

In Hafer's eyes, step one is figuring out which activities are actually valued by the end customer. You need to take into account stakeholders' concerns and requirements along the way, but if you're not defining true value in the end customer/patient/consumer's eyes, you're looking through the wrong lens.

With that in mind, more on your options:

Do well yourself

These are the things your end customer values most. You're going to say no and downplay, delegate, cut back, and avoid other things so you can spend more time on these critical activities. This is where you and your team need to strive for perfection. Doing well is an understatement. Here's where it's essential to do your absolute best.

Do yourself, but just well enough

You accept the need to do these things yourself. But they are not as important as some others. So, you should do them and do them well enough to satisfy the stakeholders that need them to fit into what they are doing for the end customer – and no better.

Delegate and supervise

The items you delegate and supervise are important. You want them done well, but there isn't enough value in doing them yourself. Or perhaps, there are others who can do the work better than you. Either way, you care about these items enough to supervise the work.

Delegate and ignore

Items you delegate and ignore are off your plate. You hope the people you delegate to will do them well, but they don't matter as much as other tasks. You're prepared to accept whatever results come to fruition.

Do later

Things you decide to do later may get done eventually, but certainly not now. They are one step above the bottom rung and delaying them may cause stress with the people who need them now. That's a choice you've made in pursuit of the highest value adding activities for the end customer.

Do never

Not only do you think these tasks are bad ideas for you and for people you might delegate to, but you also believe they are just bad ideas. Here's your clearest "no." Not me. Not others. Not anyone. Not now. Not ever. Go away. (Harsh, but clear.)

The next time a task arises, ask yourself about the end value and then determine the best approach.

The general prescription is to spend 20-30% of your time as a CEO managing up, 20-30% of your time managing out, and less than 50% managing down.

Up – This is about investing time to strengthen one-on-one relationships with individual board members, shadow board members lurking behind the visible board members, and investors. You work for them. Get to know them. It's worth 20-30% of your time.

Out – This about anticipating risks and opportunities. You need to be the one asking "What if?" Ideally, you'd have some disrupters, rebels, challengers, and deviants on your leadership team keeping you honest. Whether you have them or not, spend 20-30% of your time out with customers, collaborators, competitors and influencers of your social, political, regulatory and economic conditions.

Down – The trick here is to limit the amount of time you spend working in the business to less than 50% of your time. This means you're going to have to do less yourself and delegate more.

The thing you can't ever delegate is inspiring others with your vision and values. Purpose, frameworks and incentives can help systematize your influence. Purpose drives emotion – why. Frameworks drive thinking – how. Incentives drive action – what.

Purpose

Leadership is about inspiring and enabling others to do their absolute best together to realize a meaningful and rewarding shared purpose. People don't commit to leaders, organizations or even teams. They commit to causes. When a cause-focused purpose is genuinely shared, all understand why they must do what they are setting out to do.

Purpose inspires emotional commitment.

Frameworks

Frameworks are the basic conceptual structures that people use to flesh out their ideas. They help people know where to start, and they focus and guide thinking about how to achieve purpose.

For example, jury instructions give juries frameworks for their thinking. As US Legal explains, a trial judge gives the jury instructions to "apply the law to the facts as he gives it to them; they are not to substitute their own judgment as to whether a different law should be applied or whether the law as has been explained to them is unjust."

Frameworks are swim lanes for thinking.

Incentives

There's an old saying, "Show me how they are paid and I'll tell you what they do." Incentives are the consequences of behaviors. If the incentives are clear up front, they serve as antecedents, prompting the behavior. Even if they are not clear, people figure them out eventually.

A guy from the corporate headquarters was out with a salesman and watched him close a big sale.

"Do you know that we lose money on every case you sell at that price?"

"I do."

"Then why did you sell them so many cases?"

"I'm compensated based on revenues, not profits. I assume some genius at the corporate headquarters knew what they were doing when they put this price on this product. If you want me to focus on profits, give me the tools I need and compensate me based on profits."

Incentives drive behaviors.

If inspiring is the first part of managing down, enabling by linking and integrating efforts is the second part. This is about delegating – but still digging deep from time to time to understand your people and their potential.

One CEO Boot Camp attendee had recently taken over a new organization. He told his direct reports that he wanted them to "own" their areas of responsibility, but keep him "informed."

A few weeks later, the head of marketing scheduled a meeting to bring her new boss up to speed. She was proud of what her team had accomplished and brought a dozen of them to the meeting.

They took the CEO through their work. He probed along the way. At the end he said "I love it. Go for it."

What had he done wrong?

It's in the words.

Still don't get it? I'll give you a hint. The marketing people were so excited about how positive the meeting had been that word spread like wildfire. Every other function wanted to schedule similar meetings. The CEO's calendar got full and meetings became harder and harder to schedule.

The trouble was that day-to-day operations ground to a halt. No one would do anything until they had "informed" the CEO.

What had he done wrong?

He'd said "Go for it."

Those three words changed the definition of "inform" from conveying information to getting my approval.

If he wanted his direct reports to "own" their areas, he gave up the right to say "Go for it." Instead, he should have said "I love it. How can I help?" That would have left them in charge and given them permission to direct him to help link and integrate efforts across functions.

You

Accelerating through strategic inflection points requires step-changes in strategy, organization, and operations, carefully synced together. Those are necessary, but not sufficient unless you reinvent yourself as what John Hillen and Mark Nevins describe as a more sophisticated leader.[11]

As we've seen, one of two things gives you the opportunity or need for a strategic inflection: a change in your environment or a change in your own mission, vision, objectives or goals. Whatever creates the opportunity or need, it's going to require step-changes in your strategy, organization, and operations - in all three at the same time.

And it's going to require a different type of leader to make that happen. That different type of leader could be someone new or it could be a reinvented you.

In their book, _What Happens Now?_ Hillen and Nevins argue that doing more of the same thing requires increased capacity or complexity while doing different things requires new capabilities or sophistication. If you're growing steadily, you can probably get away with evolving your mechanics, structure, processes, and systems with your technical and functional knowledge. But, leading through a point of inflection requires new mindsets, capabilities and behaviors leveraging political, personal, strategic and interpersonal strengths.

Fitting their insights into the five BRAVE questions yields this.

Environment – Where play

Hillen and Nevins ask why leaders fail to overcome stalls of poor story/narrative, alignment, influence, explaining and leading change, authority, focus, and leadership development. Their overarching premise is that failing leaders add more complexity while more successful leaders add sophistication.

---

[11] From my May 15, 2018 Forbes.com article, _Reinventing the Missing Piece (You) in Leading Through a Point of Inflection_

Values – What matters and why

Hillen and Nevins explain how the strongest leaders do a better job telling the story with a narrative that others can believe, follow and relate to still others in different ways. That story is anchored in vision, mission and values and flows through to strategies. They suggest it needs to be clear enough for your grandmother to be able to tell it to someone else over the kitchen table.

Attitude – How to win

Hillen and Nevins make a strong case for the importance of aligning all around the strategy and culture. You can't pivot with a bunch of "freelancers" looking out for their own or their sub-groups' interests. Leading through a point of inflection requires moving from being a working group to a high-performing team.

Relationships – How to connect

Hillen and Nevins devote much of their book to the relationships required to lead through points of inflection.

When it comes to stakeholders, job #1 is to take them into account and pay attention to the range of stakeholders from customers to collaborators to competitors to those in various roles around your organizational space. Understand their relative power and interest in what you do.

With both internal and external stakeholders, it's essential to explain the change you're making, why you're doing it and how you're doing it over and over again.

This is only going to work if you continue to deserve the authority to lead. You must continue to be credible, reliable, faithful and selfless; and become ever stronger as a strategist/systems thinker. Finally, in terms of relationships, you can't do it on your own. You must invest in developing other leaders.

Behaviors – What impact

Hillen and Nevins are cognizant of the difference between doing, managing and leading. If the doers are hacking a trail through brush, the manager is helping them do that as effectively and efficiently as they can, and the leader is the one who climbs the tree to look out and point the way forward. To make the impact required to lead through a point of inflection, you have to put down your bush hacker and climb the tree.

Make your impact through coaching and developing, managing stakeholders, initiating important conversations, listening with empathy and perception, broadcasting a vision with clarity and purpose, shaping strategy to lead change, and providing others with feedback, support, and opportunities to grow.

The Fundamental Difference Between Leading and Managing: Influence Versus Direction[12]

Leaders influence. Managers direct. While it may not be that black and white, leaders generally do focus on what matters and why as managers focus on how. Both use different forms of influence and direction at different times. But leaders have a bias to influencing by inspiring and enabling through advice and counsel while managers have a bias to command and control.

Coca-Cola's Doug Ivester was crystal clear on the difference. Sometimes he'd come to us and say,

> *This is your decision to make. I'd like to give you my thoughts as input.*

Since he was the CEO, we always considered his thoughts. Most of the time we did things the way he suggested. Sometimes we disagreed. We quickly learned that going back to the CEO and telling him that we decided he didn't know what he was talking about did

---

[12] From my November 24, 2015 Forbes.com article, *The Fundamental Difference Between Leading and Managing: Influence Versus Direction*

not make for pleasant meetings. But it did work when we went back to him and said,

> *Wanted to follow up on the decision we made on this subject. After we talked to you, we did some more digging and uncovered five things that you could not have known about. Given those new findings, we decided to go a different direction than what you had suggested.*

He was fine with that.

Other times he'd say,

> *See these stripes. I am the CEO of this company. I'm going to give you some direction which you will follow.*

It was extraordinarily helpful to know when he was giving us input for us to consider in our decision and when he was giving us no choice but to follow his direction.

Decision versus input

The more companies I help with their executive onboarding and transition acceleration, the more I'm becoming convinced that clarifying decisions versus input solves a whole host of other problems.

The most important thing for any two people to clarify as they are working together is which of them is going to make which decisions at any point in time so they know when they should be deciding and when they should be providing input into the others' decision.

Decision versus input for partners

In any organization, there are natural (and unnatural) partners. It's helpful for these partners to be clear on which of them is deciding and which of them is influencing which decisions.

Take the case of a magazine publisher and editor-in-chief. They must work together as partners and communicate all the time. In general, it seems to work best if the editor-in-chief advises on marketing and pricing while the publisher makes those decisions. Conversely, the publisher should advise on content while the editor-in-chief makes those decisions.

RACI

Many have found the RACI framework helpful:

Approving Authority   Passes accountability on to someone else, retaining approval/decision rights.

Accountable: Does defined work
(and signs off on their portion of the work).

Consulted: Provides input (to be considered) and/or direction (to be followed) - Two-way conversation.

Informed: Kept up-to-date - One-way communication.

Support: Assists in completing the work

Note the accountable person may answer to a higher approving or commissioning authority that delegates the task or project to that accountable person. RACI applies within the task or project.

Implications for you

Think input versus decide. For each important decision, clarify who makes the decision and who is providing input to the person making the decision and be explicit about which you are doing at any point in time.

Separately, Sibson's Howard Fluhr told the group, "There are two types of people in any organization: the CEO and everyone else." (He went on to say that salespeople were so different that he wasn't sure they could be considered people at all.)

If everything communicates, and it does, it's even more so for CEOs. People watch everything CEOs do and don't do, say and don't say so they can figure out what the CEO is thinking, feeling, and really caring about. The life of a CEO is lived in a fishbowl.

One recurring theme then is that CEOs must be deliberate and intentional about every single interaction. You can ruin someone's day by simply walking past them on the sidewalk and not seeing them. It's not fair. But it's true.

Your role is no longer that of the hero winning the day. You're not even the captain, pulling the team together at the height of the conflict. You're the general, arranging forces before the battle.

As the general, you have to own vision and values – purpose. You have to own the strategy, and culture, and over-arching organizational and operational direction. You have to be the chief enabler, enforcer, enroller, or customer experience officer as appropriate.

Beyond 10,000 Hours: The Constant Pursuit of Mastery[13]

Robert Greene's new book "Mastery" makes a compelling case that mastery is earned, not granted. He describes three distinct phases of the journey, I) Apprenticeship, II) Creative-Active and III) Mastery. For leaders, it's valuable to apply this thinking to their own quests – particularly keeping in mind the goal is not to become a master, but continually to pursue mastery with a purpose. Three suggestions for ongoing success:

1. Embrace your own unique talent
2. Develop it into a strength
3. Devote yourself to a cause

If mastery is your end point, when you get there, you are done. You are at the top, the pinnacle, the peak. However, as Darwin told us, survival of the fittest is about survival of those best able to adapt,

---

[13] From my February 11, 2008 Forbes.com article, *Beyond 10,000 Hours: The Constant Pursuit of Mastery*

and adapting is a continual process. That's why achieving mastery is so dangerous. The only way to go from the peak is down. The moment you think you have arrived, you begin to atrophy and decline. As others adapt and move past you, your chances of survival diminish. Thus, the pursuit of mastery is a never-ending quest.

Crossing Greene's ideas (including his portrayal of Darwin) with Malcolm Gladwell's in "Outliers," Marcus Buckingham and Curt Coffman's in "First Break All the Rules," and my own thinking leads to three prescriptions.

1) Embrace your own unique talent

We all have talents. Buckingham and Coffman describe talent as "a recurring pattern of thought, feeling or behavior that can be productively applied." Greene rejects the notion of natural talent or brilliance and suggests what really matters is our innate preferences for particular activities or subjects of study. He describes how a number of masters discovered their own talents and passions. It reminds us, we are all different.

We each have unique talents or preferences and success is going to be much easier if you build off your own strengths instead of fighting them or concentrating on your weaknesses.

There is no way anyone can become a concert violinist without talent. But talent is not enough. You must acquire knowledge and skills. Knowledge comes from study. Skills come from practice. Gladwell suggests that becoming an expert or master requires 10,000 hours of deliberate practice.

This is where Greene's notions of Apprenticeship and Creative-Active come in. These are the phases Greene's masters went through between embracing their own talents and becoming masters. They learned from others and practiced their skills as apprentices: observing, practicing, and experimenting - ideally under the tutelage of a mentor. Then they went beyond what they had been taught to create new knowledge and new skills in their creative-active period.

3) Devote yourself to a cause

The most inspiring causes are unending. As Greene describes, what drove Albert Einstein was "a fascination with invisible forces that governed the universe;" what drove filmmaker Ingmar Bergman was "the sensation of animating and creating life;"and what drove musician John Coltrane was "giving voice to powerful emotions." No one masters the universe, life or emotions. They pursue understanding, sensing and creating.

The pursuit of leadership mastery

Leadership is about inspiring and enabling others to do their absolute best, and together, realizing a meaningful and rewarding shared purpose. People will follow someone who takes them to a happy place in a happy way. But they will devote themselves to the cause of a BRAVE leader who helps them make sense of their behaviors, relationships, attitudes, values and environment. It's not about you. It's not about your talents or your strengths. It's about the never-ending pursuit of learning and getting better at inspiring and enabling others to join you in a shared purpose.

When it comes to stewardship, you're the critical link between the board and organization. The most effective CEOs spend 20-30% of their time managing up, 20-30% managing out to customers and the community and less than 50% managing down. You'll need strong lieutenants.

Most of us are unbalanced – stronger in some areas than others. If you are relatively weak on the strategy side, get a strong chief strategy officer. If on organizational/people stuff, get a strong chief human resource officer. If operationally, get a strong chief operating officer. And if you are one of those rarely balanced leaders, get a strong chief of staff to give you leverage across all the areas.

With the leverage those lieutenants give you, you can focus on the most important aspects of inspiring and enabling others.

Begin with the end in mind, the last word of that thought – purpose. It's the one thing you can't delegate. If you don't believe in the organization's purpose, you're in the wrong organization. You can't fake that. "Be. Do. Say." Starts with believing.

Everything about your communication, every time, all the time has to inspire. The original definition of inspire was "to breath life into." That's your #1 job, to breath your belief in the purpose into everyone in the organization. That needs to underpin all your communication.

Your organizational or people processes are all about enabling. The objective is to get the right people in the right roles with the right direction, tools and support to be able to do their best together.

???

Boot Camp question for you to consider:

What impact? What must you do and how must you lead differently?

???

CEO Discussion Points:

The #1 job of a CEO is to own the vision and values – purpose. CEOs at CEO boot camps get that. It is about inspiring and enabling. Not surprisingly, a lot of what people said they were going to do differently tomorrow was related to vision, values and culture.

<u>Values</u>

"Focus even more on **purpose and cause**. How different people receive what I believe is the purpose and cause.

"You cannot delegate values.

"Need to "Dream big" like Rudy Karsan suggests, getting and creating a deeper sense of why.

"Will "stand in the results" (helping others envision themselves in the future instead of trying to get people excited about my vision. This was a truly wonderful addition by one of the participants who must remain nameless under Chatham House Rules.)

"Love the three goods (Happiness is good, three goods: good for others, good for me, good at it). Really brought it home for me. Got to get all three to get to greatness.

"Create a **cause** for employees to rally around.

"Need to commit to "communizing" purpose and rallying others around it.

"Better define and communicate our value proposition.

"Loved the story about the engineer who created a video to show his colleagues how their actions ladder up to making a big impact on the world.

"On plane home will think deeply and decide how to get employees to deeply engage with our mission (loved Stanley Cup story)." [The

Stanley Cup story is about how everyone in an organization that wins the Stanley Cup gets to have the cup for a day so they can share the experience with their family and friends. Amazingly enough this provides a small army of NHL people steady work repairing the cup.]

"I'm going to ask people what is our mission, why here? I need to understand where their heads are at."

"Need to work on our vision. Will implement with my team."

"I will re-look at our core values (I don't know what they are)."

It's the old brick layer story. "What are you doing?" Bricklayer #1 "Laying bricks." Bricklayer #2 "Building a wall." Bricklayer #3 "Building a school to educate our children"

Culture

"Make sure I and my team are being as BRAVE as possible – inspired with the right why – consistency of message.

"This has been a cultural re-awakening for me. Do we live by what I say: performance, discipline, respect...? Are we living this code of ethics or is it just something on the website?

"BRAVE (cultural framework) is very useful. Have each one of us give us a grade on each element: environment, values, etc. Talking about values and holding people accountable."

"On our next acquisition I must spend 45 days on cultural due diligence. It's not all about the spreadsheets."

"Play in an industry in shambles – Gave me hope and pointed out the opportunities – the place you play in reinvigorates.

"Being cognizant of when I'm "undelegating" consciously and unconsciously

"Ask who is the right person to do or decide something (other than me)

"Concentrate on only 1-2 really big things.

"Focus more on the 1-2 things that can make a difference (and focus less on the other 100 things.

"Stop bloody interfering in all departments. Stick to knitting on strategic parts.

"Ask "What do you need me to do to help you?

"Work _on_ the business, not _in_ the business

"Delegate even more (other than strategy, values and people)

"Take time to ask myself the kinds of questions we've been asking ourselves here today – especially around BRAVE and what, how, and why – challenging myself and the team.

Module 2: Stewardship

Ultimately, you are stewarding the organization for others, whether they are public shareholders, private owners, a set of people in need or fans of your team. In many cases, those people are represented by a board. Be clear on the type of board you really have. It's all about who makes decisions.

- A true **board of directors** (whether the company is public or private) has fiduciary responsibilities to those it represents and makes decisions on behalf of <u>all</u> of them.
- A **representative board** looks like it's making decisions, but is generally conveying decisions made by the specific equity owners it represents.
- A **board of advisors** provides input into the CEO/owner's decisions and doesn't even pretend to make decisions.
- **Non-profit** board members serve different roles across governance, getting or giving money, representing stakeholders, making connections, or contributing advice or time.

The CEO is the critical link between the board and the organization. The more experienced CEOs get, the less they do themselves. Delegating helps others learn and frees up CEOs' time to focus on three key processes: the strategic process, the organizational process and the operational process. Both the organization and the board have the same core processes. They are separate, but linked and wrapped in governance and culture.

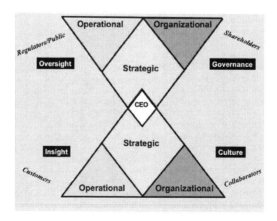

Strategic Process: Drive clarity on the board's role and its members' interactions with the CEO, senior leadership and organization. Strategy is about the creation and allocation of resources to the right place in the right way at the right time over time. The board needs to be aligned both around the strategy for the organization as a whole and its own board strategy.

As Mark Anderson points out, boards are often not clear on their purpose. When that happens they run the risk of doing a ritualistic ticking of the boxes versus taking a more disciplined approach to creating value.

Marakon's Neil Kissel preaches the need for a fundamental alignment of strategy, resources and value creation. Strategy is about choices. The choices are real until resources are moved. And it's all for naught if the outcome doesn't create value.

Operational Process: Clarify how your main board, board executive committee and board sub-committees will operate. This requires choices around decision-making, responsibilities, and groups' meetings and cadence. Often main boards follow the same cadence as senior leadership teams, tackling talent in Q1, strategy in Q2, future capability development, succession and contingency planning in Q3 and the next year's operating plan in Q4.

On the most effective boards, much of the board work happens outside normal meetings. Board members' probing, learning, discussing, and challenging outside meetings set up more productive meetings.

Mark Anderson suggests a good measure of a board's operational effectiveness is how time is used in meetings.

- Most boards devote 60-70% of their meetings to going through presentations. On the most effective boards that's under 10%

- Chairs of most boards speak 50% of the rest of the time. The most effective chairs speak less than 20% of the time.

- The most effective boards push hard for a diversity of inputs. That means that have to manage a diversity of styles – which they do.

Organizational Process: Make your board ADEPT, acquiring, developing, encouraging, planning and transitioning board members.

- Acquire board members with complementary strengths and invest in onboarding them on to the board so they can become contributors faster.

- Develop your board members' knowledge of the business context, industry and organization over time.

- Encourage board members with the right objectives and goals and then consequences of their work. Having a board performance management system enables needed transitions.

- Plan the evolution of your board over time.

- Transition board members out as appropriate. Performance management and term limits can make this easier.

Learning and communication: Enable board members to decide and advise by communicating with them in the right way. You can keep them in the dark by not giving them enough information or by giving them too much information to digest. Have a continual flow of communication with board members in one-on-ones, small groups and the like. Give them things to read and digest well in advance of meetings and include executive summaries that highlight the main points and what you need from them.

How Boards and Management Best Create Value Together[14]

At their core, boards of directors provide oversight, approve the most material decisions and advise, while management has accountability for strategy, operations and the organization. The best

---

[14] Adapted from my April 29, 2015 Forbes.com article, *How Boards and Management Best Create Value Together*

do these together, complementing and supporting the other's roles and strengths. So easy to say. So hard to get right across different types of boards and organizations.

Board Accountabilities and Responsibilities

As a general principle, a board of directors of a for profit company in the United States is charged with "maximizing the value of the corporation for the benefit of its shareholders." Boards do this by making decisions and providing oversight in compliance with the directors' duty of care and duty of loyalty. Essentially this means board members must exercise good business judgment in the best interests of the organization across governance, strategic, organizational and operational areas without regard to personal gain as they:

- Set broad policies and objectives and oversee rigorous processes taking into consideration compliance, finance, management, legal and risk issues. (Governance)

- Approve strategic plans, major expenditures and transactions, and the acquisition or disposal of material assets or the entity itself. (Strategic)

- Hire and fire the CEO. Approve top management appointments and succession, and compensation plans for the CEO and top management. Evolve and strengthen the board itself. (Organizational)

- Approve plans to obtain required financial resources, annual plans and budgets and oversee efforts to sustain and enhance the organization's public image. (Operational)

Pulling this together and building on Howard Fluhr's perspective on where boards should have their "noses in" and "hands out" yields this board management framework.

Board Management

Board Roles:
- Accountable for governance and oversight (noses in.)
- Approve strategic, annual operating (P&L, cash flows, balance sheet), future capability, succession, contingency and compensation plans.
- Advise on everything else (hands out.)

CEO Role:
- Accountable for strategic, operating, organization plans/results, culture.

Board Management:
Lead Director/Chair accountable for ("owns") board management
- Operations (committees) & board organization.

CEO responsible for board management ("does the work")
- Prepare/brief in advance, manage meetings, follow-up.
- Manage board, group, one-on-one, board two-step (Step 1: Test or consult. Step 2: Sell.)

Applicability Across Different Types of Boards

Public boards represent the shareholders of public companies. They are subjected to the strictest regulations and scrutiny and spend most of their time as boards involved in oversight and decision-making. Management needs to give members of these boards what they require for oversight and decision-making and then to implement.

Private fiduciary boards represent the owners of non-public companies. While they are not subject to all the public regulations and scrutiny, they are subject to many of them and must provide oversight and decision making in the interests of all the owners.

Private non-fiduciary boards primarily have advisory and oversight roles as the controlling owners maintain the fiduciary responsibility. Those owners may be private equity firms, families, or individuals and their organizations may be operating with different levels of maturity and different issues and opportunities. Care should be taken lest the "directors" take on fiduciary duties. Management needs to pay attention to the shadow boards behind the official boards to make sure they are implementing the right decisions.

Non-profit boards serve different roles in addition to their fiduciary duties potentially including fund-raising, contributing personal time, making connections for the organization with strategic partners and acting as advisors or representatives of critical stakeholders.

???

Boot Camp question for you to consider:

What type of board do you have?

???

Creating Value Together

As PrimeGenesis partner Rob Gregory says "If management and the board are on the same page with a shared vision as the underlying foundation for understanding respective roles and responsibilities, most relationship issues can be managed." That shared vision of what will happen and when helps clarify when board members are making decision, overseeing and supporting and when, why and how management need to provide board members with the tools and support they need to do so.

In the best value-creating partnerships, management appreciates its board members' oversight, approval and advisory roles and provides those board members with the information they need to do those well. For their part, board members are careful not to confuse oversight, approval or advice with delegated accountability and responsibility and let management manage.

With that in mind, ideal boards' composition complements management's strengths in leadership and industry and functional expertise across technology, intellectual property, finance, audit, human resources (including compensation and benefits), risk management, marketing, government relations and geographic/global perspective. Arguably some of the most material assets boards can acquire, develop and dispose of are the board members themselves.

The key to best creating value together is the partnership between the board and management. So:

1. Ensure everyone shares the same vision of success, major milestones and end-game timing.
2. Clarify roles, responsibilities, interdependencies, hand-offs and how best to operate together.
3. Assemble and nurture complementary strengths on board and Management teams.

Dividing Responsibilities Between Chair and CEO[15]

There no single right way to divide responsibilities between owners, chairmen, CEOs, COOs and the rest of the executive team. Authority is delegated. That delegation is dependent upon the business context and confidence the leaders have in one another.

Having said that, Rita's Italian Ice and Falconhead Capital – the investment firm with a controlling interest of the company – have a pretty good working model. Rita's Executive Chairman of the Board Mike Lorelli explained to me how they've broken down the roles:

The executive chairman takes the lead on:

- Running the board of directors
- Dealing with external funding (investors and lenders)
- Joint venture pursuits and relations
- Compensation practices
- Management development
- CEO succession
- Strategic plan guidance

---

[15] Adapted from my August 28, 2013 Forbes.com article, *The Right Way to Divide Responsibilities Between Chairman and CEO*

The CEO takes the lead on running the company, across its:

- Strategic process
- Operating process
- Organizational process

But that's just at this moment in time. Back up a couple of years. Falconhead Capital's CEO, David Moross, recruited Mike Lorelli to represent Falconhead on the board of Rita's. Once he understood what was going on, Lorelli started recruiting for a new CEO for Rita's in March 2013 while the old CEO was still in place. As one of PrimeGenesis' partners, Rob Gregory puts it, *"Never fire anyone until you know who's going to do their job."*

Great theory. As the situation dictated, Lorelli needed to change out both the CEO and CFO in June. So he jumped in as interim CEO.

A month later, Lorelli met Jeff Moody and they hit it off as only two ex-Pepsi employees can do. After several long conversations, a double date, and walks in the woods a la Jobs and Scully, during which they "nurtured" their relationship, Moody came on board as CEO.

Lorelli had been conscious about managing his own transition from interim CEO to executive chairman. As soon as Moody joined, Lorelli immediately vacated his CEO office and moved to an office as far away from Moody as possible. He'll back off even more over time as both he and Moody become more and more comfortable in their roles.

Lorelli said, *"The roles of executive chair and CEO should not just be additive but synergistic as well."* It's essential to have clear lines of authority. It's even better when the two share chemistry and can bounce ideas off each other. Moody described the split as *"a soft division"* with clear categories of responsibility, but major overlaps as partners.

When it works, it works great. Think about how Gates backed off and gave Steve Ballmer room to run Microsoft. Think about Ajay Banga's transition into Mastercard. But when it doesn't work, the pain and suffering are spread across all of those people who are trying to follow their leaders. If leaders can't sort through their own responsibilities, they have no chance of providing clear direction to anyone else. And don't kid yourself. There are no secrets in any company (no matter how large or small).

In summary, here is a rough guide for dividing responsibilities between an executive chairman and CEO:

1. Owners delegate authority to boards.
2. Chairs or lead directors run boards. (This is the only responsibility of a non-executive chair. Executive chairs are employees of the companies by definition and take more active roles in supporting the CEO's leadership of the company).
3. CEOs run companies.
4. COOs, CFOs, CHROs and others help CEOs run core operating, strategic and organizational processes.
5. People lean in or out depending on their confidence in the ability of the people they have chosen to deal with.

Treat this as a general framework. What really matters is clear leadership that inspires and enables others. Titles don't matter. Formal divisions of responsibility don't matter. Behaviors, relationships, attitudes, values and the environment matter. Focus on these at every level and every interaction in the organization.

???

Boot Camp question for you to consider:

How should you evolve your board – members, structure, processes?

???

Executive Chairs[16]

Generally, the chair or lead director runs the board and the chief executive runs the company. An executive chair has a potentially confusing foot in both camps, running the board and directly supervising the CEO. In DowDuPont's case, Jeff Fettig took over on April 1 as "non-employee Executive Chairman". Not joking. This does however reflect the temporary nature of his real job leading into the coming three-way split – setting the new companies and CEOs up for success.

In general:

- The CEO is an employee.
- The chair is not an employee. If the CEO is also the chair, there should be a non-employee lead director.
- An executive chair is an employee, suggesting the need for a lead director as well.

Thus, "non-employee Executive Chairman" is a contradiction in terms.

Executive onboarding is the key to accelerating success and reducing risk in a new job. People generally fail in new executive roles because of poor fit, poor delivery or poor adjustment to a change down the road. They accelerate success by 1) getting a head start, 2) managing the message, 3) setting direction and building the team and 4) sustaining momentum and delivering results.

In Fettig's case, his personal risk pales in comparison to the risk to the three new companies. In many respects, his real job is to set up for success the new CEOs of DowDuPont's three spin-offs: Corteva Agriscience, Specialty Products, and Materials Science. These are going to be brand new corporations with $15B+, $20B+ and $45B+ in revenue on day one. Fettig needs to oversee the set up of three new boards, hopefully following generally accepted practices and roles:

---

[16] Adapted from my April 5, 2018 Forbes.com article, *Executive Onboarding Note: DowDuPont New Executive Chairman Jeff Fettig's Real Job*

That should generally work for the three new boards, the three new board chairs and the three new CEOs. On the way, Fettig is partly acting as midwife to the birth of three companies and he's partly providing them air cover. His role is guaranteed to be challenging, confusing and ever-changing. It's best to ignore his title and not worry about division of responsibilities at any given moment. Instead, he should concentrate on helping the new CEOs work through the four main steps of executive onboarding:

Get a head start

DowDuPont has been planning these splits for years. Now it's time for each of the new executive teams to come together and get a head start on their own plans, on their own set up and on building their own relationships with each other and their employees.

Manage the message

Each new executive team needs to get aligned around its own core message and key communication points.

Set direction and build the team

Some sub-teams will change some will not. In a merger, acquisition or spin-off, every employee has the same question: "What does this mean for me?" Nothing else can happen until the new leadership answers that question. The faster they set a direction and tell people what their (new) jobs are, the better.

Sustain momentum and deliver results

The old saying, "Be careful what you ask for, you may get it" applies to divisional leadership teams that become their own corporations overnight. They've been asking for accountability and responsibility. Now they're getting it. After all those years of blaming "them", corporate leadership, for holding back progress, they are now "them." They must inspire and enable others, put in place their own management cadence, follow through, and deliver.

Tactical Steps in Managing Boards[17]

Ken Chenault's approach to board management + Bryan Smith's approach to persuasion = the board two-step.

Bryan Smith lays out ways of persuading in "The Fifth Discipline"

1. **Tell** – I'm the traffic policeman on the corner telling you to detour right. Not a lot of discussion. I'm in charge. You are directed.
2. **Sell** – I know I'm right and am going to persuade you to buy my idea.
3. **Test** – I've got a trial balloon that I'd like to run by you. I'm interested in what you think. This encourages you.
4. **Consult** – I've got an idea that I'd like you to help me improve. I'm open to your input and this makes you feel valued
5. **Co-Create** – Let's solve this problem together, starting with a blank page as partners.

Situational Leadership

These are also five levels of situational leadership. Different leaders deploy different leadership styles in different situations. These range from command and control (tell) to partnership (co-create). The biggest difference is between leaders providing direction (tell) and input (consult or test,) with the associated difference in decision rights.

Ken Chenault's two-step approach

Former American Express CEO, Ken Chenault, liked to give his board of directors two looks at any major idea. This gave them time to reflect on the idea, talk amongst themselves and come back to him one-on-one before making a decision.

---

[17] Adapted from my January 22, 2019 Forbes.com article, *How to Dance the Board Two-Step to Increase Your Board of Directors' Leverage*

The Board Two-Step

Putting all this together leads to the board two-step. Let's begin by taking two approaches off the table. It's generally not helpful for a CEO to try to TELL their board what to do. (If you don't understand that, give me a call and we'll talk.) It's also not a good idea to CO-CREATE with the board. (They want you to lead and come to them with potential solutions and your best current thinking.)

So, we're left with consult – test – sell. Here are the steps:

- Before step one, prepare the board by giving them the appropriate amount of information in advance. Think Goldilocks: not too little and not too much.
- Step one: CONSULT or TEST with the board. Be clear you are seeking their input, not decision.
- Then, go away. Give the board time and space to mull things over and have one-on-one conversations with you.
- Step two: SELL. Lead the board through a final conversation and seek their decision.

The Goldilocks approach to board information

There are two ways to keep board members in the dark: 1) Give them too little information and 2) Give them too much information. If you give them too much information, they can't digest it, absorb it, or make any sense of it. Help them by giving them what they need – and no more – and by using a news style inverted pyramid in presenting. My earlier piece on the subject lays this out in a little more detail but think in terms of:

- Headline
- Executive Summary
- Details of what, where, when, why, who and how.

Step one: Consult or Test

If you do your job right here, your board members relax. If they know they don't have to make a decision, they can focus on helping you. Instead of your ideas being a proposal, they represent your current best thinking for others to build on – without having to judge you.

Go away

Giving the board time and space to mull things over is important. It allows them to come back to you with their real thinking or lobby each other.

Step two: Sell

Note this is "sell," not "railroad." You will have gotten input along the way. Share the concerns you've heard so the board can discuss – and then approve your proposal.

Works with senior leadership too

Although we developed this approach for boards, it works with all sorts of groups. It is a good way to separate out input from direction. Oh-by-the-way, it's almost always a good idea to clarify if you are seeking or providing input (after which the person receiving the input gets to make a decision) or direction (a decision to be implemented by others.)

???

Boot Camp question for you to consider:

What works best in influencing your board?

???

Stewarding Non-Profits

The lines between clients, employees, contractors, leadership, board members, donors, and volunteers get blurred in non-profits. People's official labels are much less important than their view of the goods.

Recall happiness is good, and actually three goods:

- Doing good for others.
- Doing what I am good at.
- Doing good for me.

Those doing good for others are most likely motivated by the non-profit's cause. They care about helping others in need. They may contribute funds, connections, ideas, or personal time.

Those seeking good for themselves may find it in the non-profit's services, in financial compensation as employees or contractors, in increased prestige or sense of self-worth based on being associated with the non-profit.

Where corporations are ultimately accountable to their shareholders, often represented by their board of directors, non-profits are ultimately accountable to the people they serve, represented by their state's attorney general in the United States.

As CEO or "Executive Director" or whatever your title is if you're leading a not-for-profit organization, you won't go very far wrong if you treat everyone as a volunteer and inspire and enable them according to their individual motivations. This is true for virtually everyone associated with the organization from clients through donors. They're all volunteers over time.

Of course, you won't go very far wrong treating everyone as a volunteer in any organization whether it's for profit or not. Everyone is a volunteer over time.

??

Boot Camp question for you to consider:

What must you do to meet the needs of your other stakeholders?

??

Institutional Trust and Societal Issues

A major part of any board's accountabilities are governance and oversight. The best way to get anyone to trust anyone else is to be trustworthy. A recent Edelman Institutional Trust Survey[18] pointed out the importance of engaging with social issues. In their words, "Investors and the public alike are looking to business leaders to take a stand on the issues of the day and fill the void left by the implosion of trust in government." You know this is a big deal with millennials.

Specifically, 76% of respondents said companies should address one or more of these issues (ranked from most selected to least;)

1. Education reform/training
2. Environmental issues
3. Free trade
4. Automation of workforce
5. Income inequality
6. Gender issues
7. Workplace diversity
8. Immigration
9. Globalization
10. Outsourcing

---

[18] Edelman Institutional Trust Survey 2017

CEO Discussion Points:

A big "ah-ha" moment for a number of CEOs has been understanding what type of board they need and have. Some without boards realize that having an advisory board can help. Some realize that their boards are controlled by others. This often happens wquity firm has a controlling interest and sends junior partners to board meetings.

Boards functioning less than perfectly often seem to do so because of a mis-alignment of board members.

This can happen when the board has representatives of different funds with different time parameters. A PE firm needing to close out its fund within 24 months may have a lower appetite for long-term investment than may a firm with five+ years left in its fund.

Alternately this happens when individual board members have different reasons for being on the board or get confused about their individual roles. Some CEO board members have a hard time shifting from leading operations to advising and directing the people leading operations.

"Redefine my strategy for growth with board

"Revise how we manage info flow to board ahead of board meetings

- pre-meetings | one-one-ones | executive summaries on each pre-read document laying out what document says and what we need from the board members | "and here's what I need from you" note going into the meeting

"Continue to leverage lead director to sort out where board is at and where going

"Start working on an advisory council - specially to get industry content advice and perhaps set up more permanently

"Long term succession planning for board

"Utilize the board two step

"Improve board meeting communications.

Module 3: People

People leadership is one of the primary ways for CEOs to instill and reinforce their vision and values throughout the organization. Even so, scaling up as CEO means making the organizational process a level three time priority – delegated and supervised. Let the HR administrators administer. Let HR managers/directors manage. And make your Chief Human Resource Officer accountable for leading your organizational processes. The BRAVE framework (Behaviors, Relationships, Attitudes, Values, Environment) may help you guide their thinking and actions.

Environment - Where to play? (Context)

Begin with future capability planning to create a picture of what your organization must look like after you scale up through your point of inflection: Specialized? Hierarchical? Matrix? Decentralized? With what leaders and associates? This creates gaps with your current reality. Think through ways to fill those gaps including:

- Developing current people by building knowledge and skills on top of their existing talents.
- Acquiring new people with the required talents relatively soon and then building their knowledge and skills through the point of inflection.
- Acquiring new people with the required talent, knowledge and skills just in time as needed.

For example, Bosch's acquisition of battery-maker Seeo.[19]

If you're not going to follow up your long-term strategic planning with future capability planning, don't even bother starting the strategic planning work. Strategy is about the creation and allocation of resources to the right place in the right way at the right time over time.

---

[19] Adapted from my September 1, 2015 Forbes.com article, *Future Capability Planning in Action: Bosch's Acquisition of Battery-Maker Seeo*

Bosch And Seeo

When I originally wrote this piece, automotive industry supplier Bosch had just announced its acquisition of Seeo, a developer of next-generation solid-state batteries. At least some like Lux analyst Cosmin Leslau suggested this "acquisition has some wrinkles that make it a risky bet for Bosch." In particular, Seeo's status was "fragile," it was "burning through cash" and had "technical issues."

Why pay real money for a questionable business?

Because it was not about the business.

Linda Beckmeyer, a Bosch spokeswoman, said that Bosch has acquired all of Seeo's intellectual property plus its research staff. That's what they wanted. Not the current business. Not the current customers. Not even the current technology. They wanted Seeo's capabilities.

You can imagine the conversations.

"We need to increase our footprint in battery development."

"With our people?"

"By buying a company with people that know this space so they can help everyone in our company up their game in this area fast."

And that's just what they did.

Future Capability Planning

This is future capability planning in action and an example of why succession planning and talent development are not enough.

Talent development is about helping your existing people obtain the knowledge and skills they need to build their natural talents into valuable strengths.

Succession planning is about identifying who is going to take your senior people's places in the future.

Both of these are tactical exercises in support of your current strategy. Both start with existing people. Almost by definition, these people were brought into the organization to help drive the current strategy (or perhaps even an earlier strategy.)

Future capability planning is the logical, essential next step in a strategic planning process. Once you identify the strategic options you are going to pursue to bridge the gap between your aspirational goals and current reality, you need to figure out how to bridge the operational and organizational gaps required by those strategic options.

Bosch needs battery capability much faster than it can train its current people to get there. Instead, it is filling its capability gap with the Seeo acquisition.

Strategic Planning – Future Capability Planning Linkage

Strategic planning and future capability planning need to be hard wired together. As soon as you've locked into your strategic priorities, your very next question should be what future capabilities are required for us to be able to deliver those priorities? Think in terms of these steps:

- Strategic priorities
- Future capabilities required by those priorities
- Existing capabilities
- Gaps

Plans to fill the gaps (human, financial, technical and operational) including:

- Current people to develop/plan to develop them
- People to recruit early on and develop/plan to develop them
- People to recruit later

Note the three ways to fill the human gaps:

1. Invest in talent development for current people
2. Recruit people now and invest in developing them
3. Recruit "fully formed" people later

Invest in Talent Development

The first approach has the advantage of leveraging your existing resources and is the least disruptive culturally. It only works if your existing people have the required talent and you have enough time to develop them.

Recruit People Now

This approach gives you the ability to recruit people with the talents you need, and then develop them. This still requires you to have enough time to develop them.

Recruit "Fully Formed" People Later

The advantage here is that you don't have to invest time developing these people. On the other hand, they are going to be more expensive and have a greater risk of cultural miss-match.

Use one or more of these approaches as you see fit. Just have a plan.

???

Boot Camp question for you to consider:

What's your approach to future capability planning?

???

Values - What matters and why? (Purpose)

The organization's mission, vision and guiding principles must guide everything related to people. A big part of this is breaking the end versus means tradeoff.[20]

The end versus means tradeoff is not a new quandary. It's been an ethical argument showing up in ideas like Utilitarianism – the greatest good for the greatest number. It's been a political argument with people like Machiavelli arguing that, "in the actions of all men…one judges by the result." It's an ongoing leadership question in terms of the tradeoff between values and results.

It's a false choice. Organizations that survive and thrive over time deliver end results with a strong, sound, sustainable culture rooted in core values and beliefs.

At one level, how to break the end versus means tradeoff is by refusing to make that tradeoff. At another level this requires two-track leadership. Lead what is required to deliver performance and end results. And lead culture in a way that no one will make unacceptable tradeoffs of means.

Carpedia's Andrew Rush took me through their alignment process, which they call "the key to predictable and more profitable results." At a high level, this includes:

1. A Management Performance System (aligning the numbers in the business.)
2. Behaviors (the concept of "Active Management" and "Active Problem Solving.")
3. Beliefs (focus on three values that drive the business and then "listen for them.")

---

[20] Adapted from my December 21, 2018 Forbes.com article, *How to Break the End Versus Means Trade Off*

Management Performance System

As Rush explained, "First, you need to clearly define for your organization what the goal is this year. Once you have that, you need to figure out how everyone in your organization contributes to that goal. This needs to be as objective as possible. Everything that cannot be measured will have a marginal level of effectiveness.

As you do this, you will naturally go from a high level, singular goal, into smaller goals. Your time horizon will go from indicators that you can measure on an annual basis, to monthly, weekly and then hopefully daily. You will have different measures in sales, marketing, accounting, operations, etc. that will all mathematically align to the overall goal."

Another way to think about this is in terms of cascading priorities, managed with different time frames at different levels of the organization:

Strategic Priorities -- multi-year impact -- track and adjust annually or quarterly.

Programs -- that move the strategic priorities forward -- track and adjust monthly.

Projects -- that make up the programs -- track and adjust weekly.

Tasks -- that make up the day-to-day work of the programs -- track and adjust daily or more frequently as appropriate.

Behaviors

Carpedia suggests these result from Active Management and Active Problem Solving. Rush explains Active Management as, "Once you have defined what the goal is and made it clear to everyone how they contribute to that goal, you now need a cadence by which you communicate it throughout the organization and follow up against the aligned plan."

Rush told me that, "When the follow up is done, there will undoubtedly be times when variances to the plan are uncovered. How leaders analyze these variances and remove problems, so they don't occur again in the future is what we call Active Problem Solving." This goes to how you're going to adjust behaviors as you track priorities, programs, projects and tasks.

Beliefs

Rush explained that, "As a leader, you have to identify the three most important behaviors that are going to drive your business forward and make these part of your core values. Once established, defined and communicated, you now need to "listen for values". In every conversation that you have with your employees you need to listen on two levels; the first is for the exchange or information, and the second is what is being conveyed done in a manner that is consistent with your core values."

Another approach to this is to be clear with all what policies and core values are mandatory, bedrock and unchangeable and what guidelines or guiding principles are open to interpretation or evolution. Sustainable alignment happens when all know their own ends, the impact of those ends and the effect of that impact on others – and when they know which policies and values to follow and which guidelines or guiding principles to evolve.

???

Boot Camp question for you to consider:

What are the three most important behaviors in your organization?

???

Attitudes - How to win? (Choices)

The choice here is about what's required for your organization to win versus its competitors. Some organizations, like Procter & Gamble in the 1980s, win by developing their own superior talent, hiring in almost exclusively at the entry level. Others, like Coca-Cola in the 1990s, win by acquiring superior talent that others have developed. Either way, make clear, consistent choices in line with]]]]]]].[21] And build an ADEPT organization by acquiring, developing, encouraging, planning and transitioning people.

??

Boot Camp question for you to consider:

How are you going to win organizationally? (Acquire, develop, encourage)

??

The days of lifetime employment are gone for most. No longer do employees commit to organizations for their entire careers. No longer do organizations commit to take care of their employees for the rest of their lives. Instead, organizations view people as assets to leverage to create value for their owners. But the new deal goes both ways. All employees are volunteers over time. Keeping them engaged requires a new employment deal.

The new employment deal involves treating everyone as though they were self-employed, working for you as contractors only as long as it's in their best interests. That means they will stay as long as they understand how what they are doing is:

- Good for others
- Leverages what they are good at and
- Is good for them.

Good for others

It's not about you. It's about the cause, the problem to be solved, the people ultimately impacted for the better. As hard as it is for the older generation to understand, the new generation is not really

---

[21] Adapted from my December 20, 2017 Forbes.com article, *How to Manage the New Employment Deal with Your Employees*

motivated by helping owners get rich at their expense. Of course, a charismatic, caring boss can instill loyalty over the short term. But over the long term, people care about making a meaningful impact on something important.

Some companies are embracing corporate social responsibility (CSR). Many use some of the profits from their main business to help society in some way. But that's inauthentic. The best organizations' main business helps society itself.

Leadership is about inspiring and enabling others to do their absolute best together to realize a meaningful and rewarding shared purpose. The meaningful purpose is what is good for others.

Good at it

A big part of enabling your employees is removing things that get in their way. The more you distract them from doing things they are good at, the less happy they are. These disablers range from asking them to do things that don't leverage their core strengths to administrative work to meetings.

Let's pause for a moment on meetings. It's almost guaranteed you have too many of them with too many people, lasting too long.

- Reduce the number of meetings. Switch your weekly meetings to monthly and your monthly meetings to quarterly. Batch subjects and meetings to cover more in each meeting.
- Reduce attendance. Let one person represent other colleagues and report back to them afterwards.
- Reduce length. Employ tight agendas to manage time.

It's always a good idea to have your employees spend more time more focused on your customers and less time talking to themselves.

Good for them

Employee happiness is dependent on their doing things that are good for others, things they are good at AND things that are good for them. Part of good for them is compensation. But pay is a hygiene factor. The real leverage is in other, non-financial benefits like the feeling of belonging, recognition and strengthening their own personal brands.

You can no longer guarantee employees' lifetime employment. But you can help them have lifetime employability. This goes to training and development. More and more companies are cutting back on training and development. Their logic is that the increase in employee turnover reduces the value of training and development. The flaw in the argument is that reducing training and development makes it harder to recruit strong employees in the first place and reduces their level of engagement even while they are employees.

Investment and engagement

As I've said before, organizations get the employee engagement they deserve. If all you need is compliance, all you have to do is things that are good for your employees. If you want them to contribute, do things that enable employees to do what they are good at (and stop doing things that get in their way.) If you want employees to commit to the cause, inspire and enable them in that direction.

Bottom line, the new employment deal runs two-ways. Be clear on what you want and what you're willing to give up to get it.

???

Boot Camp question for you to consider:

How are you going to win organizationally? (Acquire, develop, encourage)

???

Relationships - How to connect? (Communication)

Connect with different people differently depending upon who they are, how much they care, and what you need from them in terms of engagement:[22]

---

[22] Adapted from my January 18, 2017 Forbes.com article, *Why Organizations Get the Employee Engagement They Deserve*

- **Comply.** Other than those dead set on detracting, people will generally comply if they are aware of what they need to do. This can be accomplished with indirect communication.
- **Contribute.** Getting people to contribute requires their understanding. If they know what is needed, they can deliver. If they understand why it is needed, they may find ways to do even more than asked. This requires direct communication so they can ask questions.
- **Commit.** People don't commit to leaders, teams or organizations. They commit to causes, to doing good for others. This involves going well beyond understanding to belief. Getting there requires connecting at an emotional level with those who care most.

Organizations get the employee engagement they deserve because they prompt it. Purpose-driven organizations that let employees co-create the path forward get employees committed to the cause. Those that invite their employees to contribute are more likely to get those contributions. Organizations with a command and control way of operating get mostly compliant employees. And organizations that continually re-organize and do not give their employees clear direction should not be surprised if their engagement scores are low.

The prompts range across happiness, drivers and communication.

	Happiness	Driver	Communication
Committed	Good for others	Believe	Emotional
Contributing	Good at it	Understand	Direct
Compliant	Good for me	Aware	Indirect
Disengaged	Other things	Unaware	Inconsistent

Prompting Disengagement

I cited this quote before:

> *Every time we were beginning to form up into teams, we would be reorganized. I was to learn later in life that we tend to meet new situations by reorganizing...and a wonderful method it can be for creating the illusion of progress while producing confusion, inefficiency, and demoralization.* - Petronius Arbiter, d. A.D. 65 - Roman governor and advisor (arbiter) to Nero

What's most terrifying about it is that this is not a new problem. We've all seen leaders rip the heart out of organizations, close stores, eliminate projects, lay off people, put dramatically more pressure on the survivors. They change their messages continually, sometimes looking like the strategy of the month club. Then they are amazed when those left standing start disengaging.

Prompting Compliance

Sometimes compliance is what you need.

U.S. Army colonel Randy Chase visited the store on a navy ship at sea to buy a tube of toothpaste. He went to the end of the queue of people waiting to get into the store and said "good morning" to the man in front of him who took one look at him and ran away.

Colonel Chase had done two things wrong. (1) At that time, officers didn't talk to enlisted men on ships except to convey orders and (2) officers didn't wait in lines. Where the army pushes decisions down and out in line with commander's intent so people can react to changing situations in ground warfare, the navy has a strong culture of command and control to minimize the chances of devastating onboard mistakes. The army wants contribution. The navy needs compliance and has built a culture to get it.

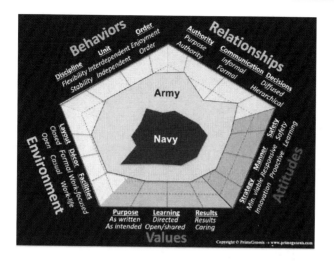

Prompting Contribution

The army promotes a culture that prompts contributions. Communication is a critical part of this. Bryan Smith laid out five methods of persuasion in *The Fifth Discipline Field* book:

Tell – Sell – Test – Consult – Co-create

If you tell someone to do something, the best you can hope for is compliance. The good news is that all you will need is indirect communication to make them aware – things like emails or corporate announcements. Just keep your message clear and consistent.

Prompting contributions requires selling, testing or consulting to help people understand what is needed. This requires direct communication so people can ask questions along the way to get at why you want something done.

Prompting Commitment

While you probably can force compliance over the short term and certainly can encourage contribution, prompting commitment is inevitably an exercise in unlocking a passion that's already there.

As Jim Whitehurst learned in his own onboarding as CEO of Red Hat, in an organization with high levels of employee engagement it's more about sparking conversations and getting out of the way. Hyper-committed people aren't going to follow your direction. They're going to do whatever it takes to drive the organization's purpose.

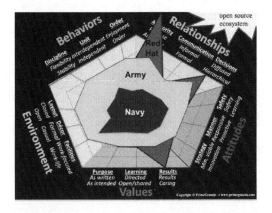

Doing good for me and doing things I'm good at matters to everyone to some degree. On top of those, hyper-committed people care a lot about the doing good for others part of their purpose. They have to believe in the cause. That's why your communication with them has to connect with them at an emotional level to change feelings.

It's why live performances have so much more impact than any note or video ever can. Magic happens when both communicating parties connect. Just as audiences get the performance they deserve, organizations get the employee engagement they deserve. If you want magic, deserve it.

Boot Camp question for you to consider:

What level of compliance, contribution or commitment are you
prompting and rewarding or punishing?

Millennials

> *"Our youth now love luxury. They have bad manners, contempt for
> authority; they show disrespect for their elders and love chatter in place of
> exercise; they no longer rise when elders enter the room; they contradict
> their parents, chatter before company; gobble up their food and tyrannize
> their teachers.*

Who said it and when? Plato quoting Socrates. This is not a new
problem. Every generation thinks the generation following it is
different. Generally, they're not.

This generation is different because of the Internet and their access to
data and information. On the one hand they can find out anything. The
see everything. On the other hand, they have been overwhelmed by this
big pipe of raw data. Many of them have spent less time filtering and
thinking about that data to turn it into information and wisdom.

Trying to keep things from millennials doesn't work. Conversations
about work/life balance have become irrelevant. The is no work time
and life time. There's just life. Trying to keep a millennial off social
media during work hours is as silly to them as trying to keep them from
thinking about work during off hours. It's all the same.

Some ideas to consider in working with, leading or being led by
millennials:

Inspire with meaning, social purpose. They are "more aware of the interconnectedness…want to understand how any business is part of this whole." They are primed to do well by doing good. Craft a future that gets them excited.

Enable them to work in their way - the main reward is respect. They are masters of digital communication. Expect multi-tasking, blurring lines of work and personal life. They've grown up with doting parents. Expect a can do attitude, seeking and giving feedback. Expect them to thrive on flexibility. Give them tasks and deadlines, not overly prescriptive step-by-step instructions.

Put them together. They are used to being parts of communities and working in teams, want friends at work and are already connected electronically with diverse people all over the world.

Behaviors - What impact? (Implementation)

Experienced leaders' #1 regret looking back on their careers is not moving fast enough on people. Figure out who is outstanding, who is effective and who is ineffective, who is in the right or wrong role to scale through the inflection and treat them accordingly[23]

When managing talent most organizations fail to differentiate. Treating everyone the same produces schools of average ducks.

An adaptation of George Reavis' fable, "The Animal School", originally written in 1940, when he was superintendent of the Cincinnati Public Schools.

"The Animal School" Fable: An Adaptation

The animals organized a school to help their children deal with the problems of the new world. And to make it easier to administer the curriculum of running, climbing, swimming and flying, they decided

---

[23] Adapted from my June 14, 2017 Forbes.com article, *The Only Six Viable Approaches to Talent Management – Invest, Support, Cherish, Move Up, Over or Out*

that all their children would take all the subjects. This produced some interesting issues.

The duck was excellent in swimming but relatively poor in running, so he devoted himself to improving his running through extra practice. Eventually, his webbed feet got so badly worn that he dropped to only average in swimming. But average was acceptable in this school so nobody worried about that, except the duck.

The rabbit had a nervous breakdown because the other animals said she looked like a rat when she jumped in the water for swimming class and all her hair got matted down.

In the climbing class, the eagle beat all the others to the top of the tree, but kept insisting on using his own method of getting there. This was unacceptable, so the eagle was severely disciplined.

And then the fish came home from school and said, *"Mom, Dad, I hate school. Swimming is great. Flying is fun if they let me start in the water. But running and climbing? I don't have any legs; and I can't breathe out of the water."*

The fish's parents made an appointment for her with the principal who took one look at her progress reports and decreed, *"You are so far ahead of the rest of the class in swimming that we're going to let you skip swimming classes and give you private tutoring in running and climbing."*

The fish was last seen heading for Canada to request political asylum. The moral of this story is:

Let the fish swim. Let the rabbits run. Let the eagles fly.

We don't want a school of average ducks.

or, **Play to people's strengths.**

Investing in Strengths

It's a lesson we learn over and over again. Most of us are unbalanced. We are relatively stronger in one area than another. There is a great temptation to fix ourselves or others by investing time to improve the areas that are relatively less strong. But that's not the way forward.

The better approach is to invest time to improve the areas that are already relatively strong, and find ways to compensate for the gaps. That could be leveraging technology or partnering with someone else. If you are relatively weak at managing operational details, partner with a strong chief operating officer. If you are relatively weak at dealing with people's problems and issues, partner with a strong chief human resource officer. If you are relatively weak at coming up with strategies, partner with a strong chief strategy officer.

Instead sort people by performance and role fit and invest, support, cherish, move up, over or out as appropriate. Expect to find most people effective and in the right role. Support them as a top priority. Then treat your other people differently, cherishing outstanding performers in the right roles and doing what it takes to help others improve their performance or circumstances.

Sort people based on performance (under-performing, effective or outstanding) and whether or not they are in the right roles.

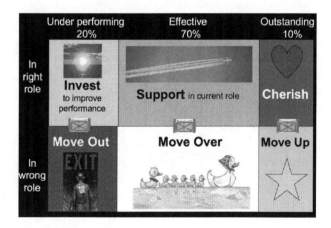

Effective in Right Role - Support

Hopefully most of your people are in the right roles and are effective. Pick your analogy. They are your girders, your backbone, your foundation. Without them, your organization won't function. You need to invest appropriately to support them in their current roles, helping them continue to grow, perform and be happy. If everyone were like them, you would not need a differential approach to talent management and your job would be easy.

Outstanding in Right Role - Cherish

A small set of your people are going to be outstanding performers in the right roles. Cherish these people. Over-invest to help them grow, perform and be happy in their current roles. The traps here are treating them the same as the first group (effective in the right role) or thinking you need to promote them. Don't do the first. These people are so much more valuable than the effective performers that they are worth dramatically more investment. Don't promote them to their level of incompetence. Not all great performers make great managers. Don't force them.

Underperforming in Right Role – Invest

The group underperforming the right role are some of your trickiest cases. The temptation is to write them off. But if you were recruiting for their replacements, you'd hire them. They have the strengths, motivation and fit to succeed. But something is wrong. Generally, it comes to poor role definition, poor direction or supervision, poor training or lack of resources. Those are fixable barriers. Do what it takes to define their roles, fix their management, give them the training or resources they need and they will perform.

Outstanding in Wrong Role – Move Up

At some point some outstanding performers outgrow their roles. You need to promote them before somebody hires them away. When that happens, you'll try to save them. Unfortunately counteroffers are almost always a bad idea. Timing is everything.

These people think they are ready for promotions before you think they're ready. If you wait too long, someone else will think they're ready. Move them up sooner than you're comfortable but with more support to succeed in their new roles.

Effective in Wrong Role – Move Over

These people are the hardest to identify. On the surface, everything looks fine. What you can't see is that they are having to work much harder than their peers to deliver the same result. It's a tribute to their motivation that they are willing to do so. But it's not sustainable. At some point they'll burn out or quit. Find them and move them to the right role before that happens.

Underperforming in Wrong Role – Move Out

The trap with people underperforming in the wrong role is trying to save them. You know they're underperforming. You just don't know if they are in the right role or the wrong role. If they're in the right role you should invest in them. If they are in the wrong role, do what you should to treat them with respect. But get them out with a minimum of discretionary investment. The #1 regret experienced leaders have looking back on their careers is not moving fast enough on their people. With people in the wrong roles move faster than you think you should to move them up, move them over or move them out.

???

Boot Camp question for you to consider:

What people moves should you make faster?

???

Acquire

There are several steps to acquiring the right people in the right way. Make sure your leaders scope roles and align all around that scope, recruiting brief, and onboarding plan, identify prospects, recruit and select, attract and onboard them so they can deliver better results faster. When you interview candidates for your most important positions, first ask them why they would want the job. Their answer tells you whether they care most about doing good for others, doing things they are good at or doing good for themselves.[24]

Start job interviews by asking candidates why they would want the job. It's the most important of the only three interview questions so you want the cleanest answer to it. Then, their answer to that first question will inform other questions you ask – if any. Their answer will let you know whether their bias is to do good for others, things they are good at, or good for themselves. Note we're talking about "buying" interviews, not "selling" recruiting or sourcing calls.

Recall the only three interview questions are 1) Can you do the job? 2) Will you love the job? And 3) Can we tolerate working with you? Or strengths, motivation and fit. Every question you've ever asked, ever been asked, or ever will ask is a sub-set of one of those three. The strengths assessment is relatively straightforward – they either have the strengths required or they do not. The fit question is tricky as you're trying to line up their personal preferences across behaviors, relationships, attitudes, values and the environment with your culture. That leaves motivation as the most important thing to get at in an interview.

Recall also that happiness is good. Actually, it's three goods: doing good for others, doing things you're good at, and doing good for yourself. Everyone operates with some balance of the three – with different biases and balances. The answer to the motivation question, "Why would you want this job?" reveals that bias:

- If they talk about the impact and effect they could have on others, their bias is most likely to do good for others.
- If they talk about how the job could allow them to leverage their strengths, their bias is most likely to do things they are good at.

---

[24] Adapted from my January 2, 2019 Forbes.com article, *Why Your First Interview Question Should Be, 'Why Would You Want This Job?'*

- If they talk about how the job could fit with their own goals or progresses them towards those goals, their bias is most likely to do things that are good for them.

Knowing that bias informs where you should go with the interview. Essentially,

- If their bias fits with what you're looking for, go on to probe strengths and fit.
- If you're not sure, dig deeper into their motivations, by going through different levels of why or impact questions until you are sure.
- If their bias does not fit with what you're looking for, end the interview. How you do this can range from going through the motions of completing the interview, to letting them ask you questions, to walking out.

Order matters. Everything you do and say biases what follows. If you start your interview by probing strengths and then ask someone why they would want the job, they may try to mold their answer to fit what they infer is important to you from your questions about strengths. They may think your question is another way for you to get at strengths. Similarly, if you start your interview by probing fit and then ask about motivation, they may try to mold their question to convince you of their fit. So, start with the motivation question – without any biases.

While the world generally needs more other focused leaders, this may not be true for your particular situation. The strongest leaders and strongest organizations over time will, indeed be other-focused. They think outside-in, starting with the good they can do for others. They are the leaders and organizations people will want to work for over time, will want to learn from, and will want to help.

Still, you may need to focus more on strengths, building required strengths to ensure your near-term survival so you can be other focused later. You may need to be a little more self-focused so you can attract and leverage people who think "good for me" first, so you can build some momentum.

The choice is yours. In any case, figuring out what drives the person you're interviewing is your most important task in an interview. Make it your first task.

Develop

Talent development should flow from your talent reviews. This is about assessing performance drivers and using a 70/20/10 approach to building skills and knowledge required for people to deliver in current and future roles (70% on the job; 20% interactions with others; 10% formal learning events). Unlike future capability, succession and contingency planning starting with the desired future state and working backwards, this starts with the current reality and builds off that.

In the movie *Whiplash*, JK Simmons portrays the teacher from hell.[25] Or is he the teacher that the best of us really needs to fulfill our potential? The question prompts a directive and another question. Directive: Go see Simmons' extraordinary performance in this film. Question: How does this apply to leadership development?

Some would argue that the highest potential rising leaders need tough love to reach their potential. Some would argue that only by pushing someone way beyond what they think they are capable of doing can you help them achieve what they are actually capable of doing. They would be wrong.

Whiplash Teaching

In the film, Simmons' character pushes students beyond the normal bounds of physical and emotional endurance. He systematically breaks down their confidence by demanding unattainable perfection and pitting them against each other. No one is sure of his own place.

---

[25] From my February, 23, 2015 Forbes.com article, *The JK Simmons 'Whiplash' School Of Leadership Development*

No one is sure of what is really expected. It's a form of emotional sadomasochism that is both horrifying and stimulating to watch.

Whiplash Leadership Development

A young man joined the State Department under Henry Kissinger. He worked on his first major report for four weeks, looking at the issue from every angle. Then he submitted the report to his boss who passed it on to Kissinger.

It came back two days later with the comment *"Completely inadequate. Redo."*

Devastated, the young man spent the next week going back to square one, re-looking at and revising everything before resubmitting the report.

It came back at the end of the day with the comment *"Still not good enough"*.

The young man worked all weekend, hardly sleeping at all. Monday morning he asked to present the report to Kissinger himself. He walked into Kissinger's office and handed him the report. Kissinger took it, looked at it, looked up and said,

"This is the third time I've seen this."

"Yes sir."

"Is this the absolute best you can do?"

"Yes sir."

"Fine. Then I'll read it this time."

It's the same story whether it's pushing a student or an employee beyond the bounds of reason. The argument is that the best respond to the challenge and the rest go away.

The Flaw in the Argument

The flaw in the argument is that motivation is inherently intrinsic. Neither Simmons' teacher from hell, nor Henry Kissinger, nor you can make anyone more motivated than they already are. All you can do is inspire and enable them. Inspire them to apply their own motivation in new ways. Enable them by getting the barriers out of their way.

Nothing Simmons' character does motivates his students. He certainly terrifies them. He certainly gets them mad. Some of them think they have to prove something to him. The most motivated think they have to prove something to themselves.

It's the same in business. Motivation and happiness comes from within.

How to Inspire and Enable People to Reach Their Full Potential

Inspiration is born of the pursuit of happiness. As discussed, happiness is good. Actually, almost everyone is motivated by a combination of three goods: doing good for others, doing things they are good at and doing things that are good for them. Thus, the key to inspiring people is helping them understand their own particular balance and which goods get them most excited. Help them see what good they can do. It's their vision, not yours.

Enabling is about leveraging strengths and removing barriers. Each of us has a unique set of talents, knowledge and skills that makes us better at some things than others. The first part of enabling has to do with identifying individuals' talents and helping them acquire the knowledge and skills to make the most of them. The second part of enabling is getting rid of the things blocking them from doing what they most want to do.

Net, don't think about motivating people. Think about inspiring and enabling them to do what already motivates them.

Encourage

Encouraging people requires clear direction, objectives, measures and support with the resources and time required for success and then recognizing and rewarding that success, leading to engaged people. But "Employee engagement" is too blunt a measure. You need to distinguish between compliant, contributing and committed people. This impacts the ABCs of people management – Antecedents (prompts), Behaviors, Consequences (positive and negative.)

We can change undesirable behavior habits. The earlier we intervene, the greater the impact. At the September HATCH Experience, neuroscientist Jeremy Richman took us through a journey of discovery about how to do this starting with the data on violence[26]. He noted that:

- 50% of the world's children will be victims of violence every year
- The same is true for one-fifth of the developed world's adults
- In the USA a violent crime is committed every 27 seconds
- There's a suicide every 14 minutes
- There's a drug overdose death every 12 minutes

But, he explained, those are just numbers – until they're not. On December 14, 2012, his daughter Avielle was one of the 20 children shot and killed at the Sandy Hook elementary school.

As a result of that, he left his corporate job and founded the Avielle Foundation to prevent violence and build compassion through neuroscience research, community engagement and education.

Through Jeremy's work there he's learned to talk about "brain health" instead of "mental illness." This is about changing labels. As he described, you would say someone "has a broken leg." You

---

[26] Adapted from my November 15, 2017 Forbes.com article, *The ABCs of Changing Undesirable Behavior Habits* (A sad note: Dr. Richman took his own life on 3/24/19)

wouldn't say they "are a broken leg." The same should apply to brain health. We should say someone "has schizophrenia," not they "are schizophrenic."

Beyond that, he has worked to bridge the gap between brain chemistry and behavior. He's learned about the advantages of early intervention to change habits. He explained that today's prison corrections departments do anything but correct. More than 70% of adults released from prison end up back in prison within five years. Intervening with adults has limited impact.

On the other hand, intervening with juveniles can have meaningful results. Interventions there have dropped the repeat, or recidivism, rate to 35%.

Of course, the best option is for families to teach their children good habits. The recidivism rate for people who never go to prison is 0%.

The earlier we intervene, the greater the impact.

Changing undesirable behavior habits at work

The pattern holds at work as well. The earlier we intervene, the greater the impact.

Michael Brown's ABCs of behavior modification provide a framework to follow. ABC stands for Antecedent, Behavior, Consequence. People do things because an antecedent prompts that behavior. They do it again because of the balance of consequences: rewarding or punishing desirable or undesirable behavior.

It's often hard to modify existing patterns of behavior because those habits have been reinforced by a poor balance of consequences. Witness film producer Harvey Weinstein's long history with the casting couch. The positive consequences of his behavior were immediate gratification and successful films. Why would he change?

Obviously, that's an extreme example. But it's almost guaranteed that people in your organization who persist in doing things you don't want them to do are having their behavior positively reinforced. If, as another example, employees habitually show up late for meetings, that behavior is likely positively reinforced by avoiding the negative consequence of wasting time for the few that do show up on time.

If you want to change undesirable behavior habits, change the balance of consequences. Make sure you are:

- Positively reinforcing desired behavior
- Punishing undesirable behavior.

Change the way you:

- Positively reinforce undesirable behavior
- Punish desired behavior

Just as the best way to eliminate recidivism in prison is to keep people from doing things that would land them in prison in the first place, the best way to eliminate undesirable behavior is to make sure it never happens to start with. This is about antecedents and prompting the right behaviors.

The organizational process is one of your three core process. Treat this just as seriously as you do your strategic and operating processes to scale up through points of inflection. If you have a strong Chief Human Resource Officer capable of partnering with you to lead people strategically and tactically, make them accountable and stay close to them. If not, make it a level one priority for yourself and do it well.

Captains

Having the right team ingredients is not enough until a leader inspires and enables the individuals to do their absolute best together as a team[27]. Having the right coach, players, money and strategy are

---

[27] From my July 11, 2017 Forbes.com article, *Why the Key to a High-Performing Team is the Captain Class BRAVE Leader*

necessary, but not sufficient until you have such a leader. The implication for you is to ensure there is a "captain class" BRAVE leader in some role on each of your most important teams, and then prompt and encourage them to do what they need to do.

In researching his brilliant book, *The Captain Class,* Sam Walker identified and analyzed 16 freakishly successful sports teams and another 100+ that were almost as successful over the past century. The common driver on the most successful teams, from Cuba women's volleyball to All Blacks rugby to French handball to the NY Yankees, was not coach, stars, money or strategy but the presence of a courageous, dogged, passionate, aggressive leader. In every case, the team's extraordinary run started when a BRAVE captain joined the team and ended when they left.

Walker looked at teams that had five or more members who interacted with opponents, competed together (unlike gymnastics or skiing), played a "major" sport against the world's top competition with sufficient opportunity to prove themselves, and dominated for at least four years with records that stand alone.

These teams had stars like Pele (Brazil), DiMaggio (Yankees) and Messi (Barcelona) who often delivered at moments of truth. While these stars got the glory or the girl (including Marilyn Monroe), they were too me-focused to lead others to extraordinary heights. It was the less skilled, less flashy team captains like Bellini (Brazil), Berra (Yankees) and Puyol (Barcelona) who inspired and enabled others to perform at their best together through their own obsession with the whole team's collective success.

Walker highlights several attributes these captain leaders had in common that conveniently line up with the BRAVE leadership framework. The art of the general (or CEO) is arranging forces before the battle at a strategic level, starting with the question of where to play. The art of the captain is leading forces in battle tactically, dealing with questions of what matters and why, how to win, how to connect and what impact. Walker's attributes line up with these.

Values – What matters and why

Strong convictions and *courage* to stand apart and stand up for the team to anyone (starting with the conviction of the importance of the team over everything else including self).

Attitudes – How to win

Extreme *doggedness* and focus in competition almost to the point of madness – like playing through concussions (All Blacks' Buck Shelford), broken toes (USA soccer's Carla Overbeck) or even heart attack (USSR hockey's Valeri Vasiliev.)

Ironclad emotional control — including having a "kill switch" to turn off distracting thoughts - like French handball's Jerome Fernandez' father's imminent death.

Relationships – How to connect

Motivates others with *passionate* nonverbal displays — like the Pittsburg Steelers Jack Lambert's letting the blood from his hand gash smear his jersey and pants.

A low-key, practical, and democratic communication style — with a bias to private words of encouragement or correction over public speeches.

Behaviors – What impact

Aggressive play up to and often beyond the limits of the rules — including taking penalties when they lead to better results for the team - like Cuba volleyball's Mireya Luis taking trash talking to new heights against Brazil.

A willingness to do thankless jobs in the shadows of more acclaimed teammates — like carrying water or bags or cleaning up or accepting less than market value in pay to create space versus a team salary cap to bring in other players the way the Spurs' Tim Duncan did.

Implications

- Teams need stars and leaders. Don't confuse the two. Make sure you have the star designer, builder, salesperson, logistical expert or the like on the team. AND ensure there is a captain class BRAVE leader.
- Prompt them to lead — from any chair. Their title, level or formal designation is irrelevant.
- Get out of the way to let them do what they do.
- Encourage them with positive reinforcement appropriate for them.

Perspectives

Sibson's Dan Fries has been our human resource expert in the room for most of our CEO Boot Camps. He shared these thoughts and perspectives[28]:

What Are CEOs Saying About Their Human Capital Strategies? What Are Your Views?

- ➤ "People represent our greatest asset and they are the greatest performance differentiators."

- ➤ "My direct reports are steeped in the specific content of their roles (e.g., CFO, Head of Sales, etc.), but struggle when asked to step into a leadership role."

- ➤ "My people are solid with numbers, but they often lack management and people development skills."

- ➤ "If I am honest, we have moved little in assessing leadership performance, since many of the individual performance metrics remain financially based (EBITDA, Revenue). We lack alignment with our People and Customer philosophies that are touted in our mission/vision statements."

- ➤ HBR surveyed 24 CEOs at large public companies and asked what are the 3 things that they worry most about – 16 stated top worry was Talent Management

---

[28] From Dan Fries' CEO Boot Camp presentation slides.

CEO's Role in Talent Management – What the Data Suggests

BACKGROUND DATA ON CEOs AND TALENT MANAGEMENT

➢ **TIME:** Today, CEOs are spending upward of 20% of their time on talent management (TM), while larger organizations note CEOs can spend over 30% of their time on TM.

➢ **TIME ALLOCATION:** Time is being allocated in development, assessment (often more informal), mentoring (more informal), succession, and team building amongst direct reports.

➢ **SUCCESSION:** Formal succession plans for the CEO and leadership is now a mandate for Boards. This reality requires that CEOs take on a more active role in the TM for direct reports and the organization as a whole.

➢ **MISSION/THEME:** Although talent management and themes of "people are our greatest asset" are linked directly to mission, the data shows that much of the CEO's time in TM is
ad hoc and informal.

➢ **METRICS:** CEOs admit it is a struggle to think about talent and TM metrics in the same way they would address business metrics and outcomes.

QUESTIONS FOR THE GROUP

➢ Do the above link to your experiences, and if they differ, how?

➢ How do you strike the balance between the near- and longer-term talent perspectives? Do you?

➢ In the time you spend on talent for your leadership team, where do see the greatest impact?

Straw Model on a CEO's Approach to Talent Management

What follows is an approach that one CEO developed when thinking about his role in Talent Management (TM). Elements are also used with the Board and Board assessment

1. <u>ACKNOWLEDGE</u>: Acknowledge that TM is mission critical for the CEO role.

2. <u>DEFINE/SHARE</u>: Define what you mean when you talk about talent and TM in your organization and share that broadly. Is it truly a driver of performance or HR governance?

3. <u>MINDSET</u>: Create a TM mindset and "TM language" within the organization that is focused on continued development.

4. <u>STANDARDS</u>: Building on the above, define the standard of TM and focus on constantly growing the base of talent in the organization.

5. <u>INFLUENCE</u>: The CEO needs to influence people decisions and play an active role.

6. <u>PROCESS/REVIEW</u>: Develop a simple process around TM so you can review progress and consider discussing talent in an appropriate open forum.

7. <u>LEAD BY EXAMPLE</u>: This begins at the top, but ultimately, the process of TM can drive results and works best if deemed to be owned by the organization where they become the ambassadors.

CEO People Leadership

As we close out this module, remember you can't be the star player any more. And you can't even be the on-the-field captain. You have to be the general, working behind the scenes to arrange forces ahead of the actions.

Mark Anderson shared six of his insights into leadership qualities.[29]

- Your leadership self – your demeanor, tone, and values. Be intentional.
- Setting and selling a vision and strategy. Be persuasive.
- Your team is more skilled than you (in their roles.) Be humble.
- Credibility is born of repetition. Be. Do. Say.
- Performance excellence. Be intolerant of mediocrity.
- Led by customers. Be the voice of the customer.

Pearson's ex-CEO Marjorie Scardino was one of his heroes. She led for 16 years with one mantra: "Brave. Decent. Imaginative." Everyone remembered that and lived it.

Of course, different cultures have different views of what "decent" means. As a case in point, consider the differences between Henry VIII and Suleiman the Magnificent's approaches to succession management.[30]

Henry VIII and Suleiman the Magnificent were contemporaries that had dramatically different approaches to succession management. In theory, an English king had one wife whose first-born son would succeed the king. The rulers of the Ottoman empire had harems which included several concubines who could produce heirs.

The modern-day business parallels are the organization that designates one successor to its leader versus the organization that nurtures several possible successors and lets the best successor emerge.

---

[29] From Mark Anderson's CEO Boot Camp presentations
[30] From my May 3, 2012 Forbes.com article, Choosing Between Henry VII and Suleiman the Magnificent's Approaches to Succession Management

Which works better?

Henry VIII's Succession

Henry's first wife Catherine of Aragon produced no sons – divorced her. Then second wife Anne Boleyn produced no sons – beheaded her. Then Jane Seymour did produce a son, but died in childbirth. And Henry's next three wives, Anne of Cleves, Catherine Howard, and Catherine Parr produced no children. Further, none of Henry's children had children. Henry was succeeded by his son Edward who was succeeded by Mary who was succeeded by Elizabeth who was the last of the Tudor monarchs. All in, the Tudors held the crown of England from 1485 to 1603 – 118 years.

Suleiman the Magnificent's Succession

Conversely, one of Suleiman's eight sons succeeded him. Then that son's son succeeded him and so on. (Note I'm not talking about the accepted practice of the new ruler's killing all his brothers to head off any possible succession disputes.) All in, Suleiman's relatives ruled the Ottoman Empire from 1299 to 1922 – 623 years.

Harems win.

The implication for business today is that options reduce risk. Locking in on one successor reduces options and opens the organization up to the risk of choosing wrong or something happening to the chosen successor. Keeping more options open longer reduces that risk because the other possible successors are more likely to stay around and more likely to continue to be nurtured for the role.

We'll address the personal benefits of harems in a different forum – particularly now that our understanding of DNA makes male as well as female harems feasible.

CEO Discussion Points:

Experienced leaders #1 regret is not moving fast enough on people. Boot Camp attendees get that point. Many of them commit to investing more in the differential capabilities, freeing up resources by simplifying or outsourcing areas in which the can be merely good enough to invest in those very few areas in which they need to be best-in-class.

Question #1 seems to be where to play. CEOs quickly move on to the importance of culture and the need for them to build personal relationships with key people – including rising stars and people that can tell them the truth.

(Where play)

"Going to hire a chief of staff.

"Look at how committed the organization is to people development as we look at acquisitions: succession planning, development

"Invest in (future capability planning, succession planning and contingency planning) to bridge from my old ways doing things to new.

"Conduct a human resource audit (as part of acquisitions, etc.)

"Delegate more, give people more freedom to make decisions.

(What matters and why)

"Detractors and change management is the lonely part of the job.

"Conversation with HR director about assessing culture at low-performing depots.

(How win)

"Always been talking about the HR function – the most important strategic function within the business, yet one of the weakest in all our companies. Most HR managers seem to be called either Donna or Nancy. We are not going to grow and succeed without strengthening this function.

"Put in place long-term incentive plan. Want to retain our people. (In general,

- Short term salary and benefits should meet hygiene issues so people don't have to worry about their day-to-day expenses;
- Mid-term performance bonuses should link near-term consequences to near-term results;
- Long-term incentives should link long-term consequences to long-term value creation.

"Need BRAVE captains on every team.

(How connect)

"Have lunch with people three levels down. (To recognize and acknowledge top performance and create a network of spies.)

"Learn something about each player on my team, to tighten personal connections

"Relationship manager for each contractor, and align their interests with ours.

"All sorts of interesting discussion about working with Millennials who are becoming an ever-increasing proportion of the workforce. People sparked to Marco Bizzarri's idea of "Giving the same agenda to millennials and existing colleagues and testing reactions."

"In any case, some understood the need to 'Listen more and share my vision after listening, so that it is more receptive for younger people."

(What impact)

"Get the right people in the right seats on the bus. I've learned that ten times. But I haven't learned it. I always know intuitively what to do. And then I don't pull the trigger. I don't want to admit failure on my own part when I can't rehabilitate someone. Other times I value their experience. Got to get it done.

"Taking swift and decisive action. Will go forward with our RIF.

"Transition out a senior leader who is a detractor.

"Moving faster on people.

"Like the three nights of sleep guideline. (If someone keeps me awake three nights, they're gone.

"More sophisticated view on challenges in moving people from "detractors" to "watchers" (and then "supporters")

"Will move to have a mix of some new and some old people in the organization. Need to inject some new thoughts.

Module 4: Innovation

In most industries, the lowest cost player makes money selling large quantities of product or service at a low price with great discipline. The differentiated player makes money selling smaller quantities of higher quality product or service at a relatively high price fueled by value-creating innovation. Those in the middle lose. Those that break the price/quality tradeoff at scale win big.

This note suggests a BRAVE approach to scaling innovation, a cross between the ideas in Skarzynski and Crosswhite's *The Innovator's Field Guide,* with my own BRAVE leadership framework (Behaviors, Relationships, Attitudes, Values, Environment from the outside-in).

Environment - Where to play? (Context for innovation)

Start with a shared understanding of your organization's innovation needs. Webster defines innovation as "the introduction of something new." Harvard Business School's Linda Hill suggests it should be useful as well. Know the relative importance of inventing verses introducing inventions to your organization, market, world. Consider the challenge you face. Do you need revolutionary, disruptive innovation or merely to scale evolutionary, incremental innovation?

Values - What matters and why? (Purpose of innovation)

Your organization's mission, vision and principles should guide everything else you do.

Attitudes - How to win? (Innovation choices)

Aim your efforts at business concepts and models and not at just product and service inventions and improvements. There's more value in scaling innovation across the entire value chain than in one-off efforts. Look across products, processes, services, technologies and business models.

Relationships - How to connect? (Innovation communication)

As Hill says, you must "Unleash the talents and passions of the many from the stranglehold of the few". My friend Will Travis talks about the value of giving people permission to explore "in the friction zone" with problems to solve, watching them play, accumulating and collaborating to create and strengthen insights, and rewarding small wins to build momentum.

Want to prompt creativity? Make someone unhappy.[31]

If people are happy, there's no need to change. But if people are faced with others' or their own distress, they will work to find creative ways to bridge the gap from bad to good and unhappiness to happiness.

Happiness is good - three goods: good for others, good at it, good for me. This means there are three opportunities to create distress: others' distress, strengths mismatch or personal distress.

Others' Distress

Many of society's advances were born out of someone's finding new, creative ways to solve others' problems.

Fire was born out of the need for a better way to keep warm.

Vaccinations were born out of the need to protect people from diseases.

Pet Rocks were born out of the existential need for more meaningful holiday gifts.

The list goes on and on.

Einstein told us that we couldn't solve problems with the same level of thinking that created them. When some people's level of distress

---

[31] From my April 19, 2017 Forbes.com article, *Why the Route to Creativity Runs Through Distress*

with others' unhappiness reaches a breaking point, they move to new levels of thinking and create new ways to solve the underlying problems.

Prompt creativity by helping people see others' needs.

Distress from Strengths Mismatch

The world needs different types of leaders: artistic, scientific and interpersonal. Those leaders have different strengths and different ways of thinking. Some of the most creative ideas have come when those leaders are forced to think in different ways.

Doug Hall has been forcing people to do this for decades. Doug was trained as a chemical engineer and as a circus clown. He was a brand manager at Procter & Gamble, eventually becoming "Master Marketing Inventor" there before starting his company, Eureka Ranch. In its early days, Eureka Ranch drove *"creativity, stimulus and fun"* and helped all sorts of business executives play outside of their comfort zone by deploying things like Nerf guns, water cannons and whoopee cushions.

Howard Gardner suggests there are nine different types of intelligence:

1. Naturalist Intelligence (Nature Smart)
2. Musical Intelligence
3. Logical-Mathematical Intelligence (Number/Reasoning Smart)
4. Existential Intelligence (Getting at the meaning of life)
5. Interpersonal Intelligence (People Smart)
6. Bodily-Kinesthetic Intelligence
7. Linguistic Intelligence (Word Smart)
8. Intra-personal Intelligence (Self Smart)
9. Spatial Intelligence (Visual/picture Smart)

Thus, stimulate different leaders' creativity by getting them to access different types of intelligence than they normally do.

- Stimulate artistic leaders outside of their visual, kinesthetic, musical, linguistic comfort zones.
- Stimulate scientific leaders outside of their naturalistic, logical-mathematical, existential comfort zones. (Though I'm not sure anyone is ever really comfortable pondering the meaning of life.)
- Stimulate interpersonal outside of their intra-personal and interpersonal comfort zones, getting them to think like artistic or scientific leaders.

This all comes down to prompting creativity by making people think or act in new ways.

Personal Distress

Brand Communication agency Sid Lee's Will Travis will tell you that if the road to creativity runs through distress, the road to extreme creativity runs through extreme distress. Will has climbed several of the world's highest summits including Vinson Massif in Antarctica in the most brutal 45 degrees below zero Centigrade conditions imaginable, motor biked with The Paris Dakar and traversed the 18,000 Khardung La pass in the Himalayas and generally put himself in extremely stressful situations.

These experiences have helped Will both see things in different ways and keep things in perspective. As he put it,

Facing situations of life and death implications elevates one's vision way above the severity of the business landscape, resulting in both centered and humanistic decision making, that business school nor mentors can never teach.

Will uses this perspective to help the people he leads face and manage their own fears. It's painful when a client cold heartedly rejects a creative team's heart invested work. But we have to keep it in perspective that its' not a life-threatening situation. Will suggests

You have to fail…Failure puts you in a friction zone, puts you in a zone where you have to make a decision, you have to change and do something different to survive and move on.

Look at jobs to be done, domains, and innovation architecture. Manage constraints while moving from idea to business concept. As Skarzynski and Crosswhite suggest

> *"Don't start with new ideas. Start with new insights, which help you develop new and different perspectives about your particular innovation challenge."*

It is counterintuitive.[32] You would think the more scope, time and resources you have, the easier it would be to innovate. Chris Denson, Director, Ignition Factory at OmnicomMediaGroup says you would be wrong. He suggests "The more limited you are, the more creative you have to be. Time constraints eliminate second guesses. Constraint is a unifier." This may explain why larger resource-rich organizations struggle with revolutionary innovation.

Let's look at Denson's points one by one.

Mission constraint is a unifier.

HATCH's Yarrow Kraner describes the constraints adventure hostel Selina's cofounder Rafi Museri has had to deal with "to reimagine a new vertical, catering to a quickly evolving digital nomad audience, this group needed to move quickly, efficiently, and responsibly to scale at a pace that would put them on the map quickly, without breaking the bank. All of the furniture and fixtures are hand-crafted by up-cycling found trash, rubble, and debris and giving second life to previously consumed resources.

To accomplish scaling at this rate with such artisan craftsmanship, Selina's Creative Director Oz Zechovoy has been training ex-gang members to be carpenters, builders, and welders. They are quickly growing from three locations currently to 10 by the end of 2016, and

---

[32] Adapted from my March 9, 2016 Forbes.com article, *Why Adding Constraints Increases Innovation*

over 90 locations within the next 4 years, creating hundreds of new jobs and positively impacting Panama's economy."

In this case, the constraint forcing innovation is the overlapping missions: to build adventure hostels catering to the evolving digital nomad audience *and*, at the same time, to give products and people in Panama a second chance.

Time constraints eliminate second guesses.

An example of time constraints forcing innovation is found in the way NASA team members came together during the Apollo 13 crisis. Right from *"Houston, we've had a problem,"* the team reacted flexibly and fluidly to a dramatic and unwelcome new reality—a crippling explosion en route, in space.

The team went beyond its standard operating procedures and what its equipment was "designed to do" to exploring what it "could do." Through tight, on-the-fly collaboration, the team did in minutes what normally took hours, in hours what normally took days, and in days what normally took months. This innovation was critical to getting the crew home safely.

The constraint here was all about time. Not only was failure not an option, but success had to come fast. Very fast. This imperative broke down all sorts of petty barriers and got everyone rallied around what really mattered, leading to innovation out of necessity.

The more resource limited you are, the more creative you have to be.

Kraner describes Kalu Yala as an example of just this: *the world's most sustainable community - that started as a conscious real estate play, but the founder realized that it would take millions of dollars to build out a destination before attracting buyers, and flipped into an institution as it's first priority, teaching while learning about sustainable best practices.*

Can civilization and nature coexist? Can our diverse cultures coexist with each other?

The first phase, and the foundation of the plan is the Institute; an educational platform for students from around the world who are collecting, implementing, and documenting best practices in sustainable living. The work-study program has hosted students from all over the world from 25 countries and 150 colleges.

Kalu Yala's Jimmy Stice didn't set out to build an institute. But, as he put it, "Constraints are what give a design its focus and ultimately, its true shape."

Implications

Innovation requires one of the only three types of creativity: connective, component or blank page. The surprise is that these thrive on less resources rather than more. Don't over-water your plants and don't over-resource your innovation:

- Narrow and focus the mission.
- Give tight deadlines.
- Limit resources.

If you need innovation, put people in a box with limited resources and a tight deadline. The real innovators will thrive on the challenge and find surprising, new and perhaps revolutionary ways out of the box.

??

Boot Camp question for you to consider:

How do you change the context to encourage more innovation?

??

How to Tap the Only Three Types of Creativity[33]

There are three and only three ways to create. They come from connective, component and blank page creativity. That's it. Those three. If you want to *"make new things or think of new ideas"* as Webster defines creativity, you must do one of these three.

- Do you see disparate things you can pull together? That's the path to connective creativity.
- Do you see complex things you can take apart? That leads to component creativity.
- Do you see things that aren't there? That's the start of blank page creativity. (Or a new M. Knight Shyamalan film.)

At the inaugural HATCH Latin American experience in the jungle in Panama, three young women shared with us examples of the different types of creativity.

Butterscotch – Connective Creativity

Butterscotch creates music out of the same twelve notes and basic sounds everyone else uses. But she connects them in ways others do not. At HATCH we watched her loop things in real time.

First, she laid down the beat. She's a beat boxer. So, she didn't need a drum, just her vocal chords and facial muscles. Then she used her guitar to lay down some basic chord progressions and added some musical highlights that sounded like brass instruments – all with her vocal chords. With those three looping underneath in supporting roles, she sang – beautifully.

Her creative magic came in the way she connected existing ideas in new ways.

---

[33] From my March 1, 2016 Forbes.com article, *How to Tap the Only Three Types of Creativity*

Stefani De La O – Component Creativity

Stefani De La O innovates *"in the details."* Her Nomadic Collector collection of high end hand bags and luggage was born out of her need *"to see how the pieces come together"*. She studied architecture, art history and fashion design so she could do that. But it's rooted in the components.

As Stefani explained to me, her brain takes in everything. It doesn't filter out information that others see as unnecessary. To her everything matters, everything is important. She doesn't see the forest. She doesn't see the trees. She sees the veins in the leaves, the different textures in the bark, the moisture flowing up the core of the tree, the roots interacting with the life-giving soil around the tree.

She doesn't see handbags. She sees cows and cotton plants and iron ore.

It's that super power of deep insight into the components that make her creations so special.

Bethany Halbreich – Blank Page Creativity

Bethany Halbreich is a painter who sees things that simply aren't there and never have been there. She told me how she'd start a painting with a squiggle and build from there.

Bethany is not just creative herself, but the cause of creativity in others. She founded Paint the World, a nonprofit devoted to harnessing the power of "blank page creativity."

> *"Our goal is to inspire creativity and collaboration by facilitating artistic experiences in underserved communities that have little to no access to art education.*
>
> *We place large blank canvases and art supplies in these communities, and watch to see what evolves, what symbols might appear that could help us understand the unconscious undercurrent of a community. Everyone builds on each other's work. We auction the finished pieces and the proceeds always go directly back into the communities."*

There's real power here. Whatever is your preferred mode of creativity - connective, component or blank page - the multiplier is in collaboration. That was one of the lessons of HATCH Latin America, an amazing experience connecting creative catalysts to hatch a better world together.

Implications for you

Don't misread the point. You do not have to pick one route. Do experiment with the different forms of creativity. You never know what's going to happen if you push your boundaries or break out of your box. The important point is to appreciate others' modes of creativity.

It's all about collaboration. It's all about complementing your own strengths with others' strengths. Understand your own strengths. Understand your gaps. Then find others to fill them.

Managing Extraordinarily Creative People[34]

Managing extraordinarily creative people is challenging if not impossible. But you can bring out their best if you give them leverage, inspire and enable them. Their leverage comes from understanding and taking full advantage of their own natural talent, temperament and inclinations. Inspiring them is about protecting them, pointing the way forward and encouraging them. Enabling them is about giving them the resources, time and space they need to imagine, play, practice and create.

By anyone's definition, Salient Technologies' David Yakos is extraordinarily creative. Origins magazine describes him as one of its 45 top creatives and an "Inventor, maker, designer, painter, adventurer, and engineer. From aerospace to toys, he blurs the lines between art and engineering."

---

[34] From my November 2, 2016 Forbes.com article, *The Three Keys to Bringing Out the Best in Extraordinarily Creative People*

(This last piece sounds a lot like what sparked the magic at Disney's creative oasis – Imagineering.)

I've gotten to know David through several HATCH experiences and spoke with him for this piece.

Leverage

The world needs three types of leaders: artistic, scientific and interpersonal. They need to be creative themselves and bring out creativity in others. For example, David likes to "confuse the world of art and engineering." Just as he is part artist and part mechanical engineer, his product development process blends creativity and practicality "from ideation to production":

1. Conceptual design, where you explore the look and function of the concept.
2. The prototype process, where you physically and digitally test the feel and function.
3. The production design, where you communicate with the factory the design intent using manufacturing files and engineering drawings.

David's mother saw this innate talent and nurtured it. In an interview with Tanya Thompson, David described how,

My mother cut down an empty drier box, filled it with supplies including empty shampoo bottles, egg cartons, string and everything else I would need to build my first spaceship, first homemade pair of paper shoes and a cardboard robot suit. It was David's Creative Corner. I could visit that world and come back with something new, an invention that was unique and never before seen.

In line with Leslie Owen Wilson's thinking on creative traits, David has a natural curiosity, intellectual playfulness, a keen sense of humor and is aware of his own impulses.

Inspire

Extraordinarily creative people need to be protected, directed and encouraged. At the same time, Wilson suggests they need to be uninhibited and willing to take risks given their heightened emotional sensitivity and being perceived as nonconforming.

David knows that "all great businesses begin with an idea, but it takes engineering and product development to turn an idea into a reality." That's his focus and his firm's focus. And they've done well through the years, winning Popular Science's Best Prototype of 2013 and currently nominated for the Chicago Toy & Game Group's Toy & Game Innovation (TAGIE) award for excellence in toy design for David's Mega Tracks for Lionel Trains.

Enable

Enabling extraordinarily creative people is about tools and time. They need resources, connections and basic tools. And they need time to play and learn in line with Wilson's premise that the most creative go through a large number of ideas, often thriving in disorder and chaos.

David told me that *"People are almost embarrassed with their own creativity. We need to give people permission to stop being adults and engage in child-like imaginative play. It's not about learning how to be imaginative or creative. It's about never growing out of it...I live in a safe place where it is okay to have silly ideas and safe to fail as part of taking "a broad sweep of ideas, (and) polishing the best ones."*

And they need people around them with complementary strengths that can sometimes serve as the adults in the room.

Implications

1. Don't try to fix extraordinarily creative peoples' "opportunities for improvement". Help them be even better at what they are already good at.

2. Encourage them by protecting them, pointing the way forward and recognizing the cool things they come up with and do.
3. Give them the time and space they need to imagine, play, practice and...wait for it...create.

???

Boot Camp question for you to consider:

What can you do to mash up people with different types of creativity?

???

Behaviors - What impact? (Implementing innovation)

Innovation is inherently messy. Bring some order to the chaos and scale with a create – iterate – assess - implement and scale approach combining IDEO's Human-Centered Design and BAC's Scratch approaches with a heavy dose of Design-Thinking:

Create

- Prepare by learning, listening, observing patterns of behavior, points of pain and inconvenience to gain insights across five dimensions: 1) Customer insights, 2) Market discontinuities, 3) Competencies and strategic assets, 4) Industry orthodoxies, 5) Seeing and mapping white space where no one is playing.
- Generate ideas - with champions to carry them through and the right level of innovation for each initiative: 1) Acquisitions (like Ebay acquiring PayPal), 2) Sister companies (like Amazon keeping Zappos in the family but separate), 3) Separate divisions (like Disney's Imagineering or Procter & Gamble's Miami Valley Labs), 4) Skunk works (like Lockheed's Skunk Works), 5) Giving all protected time to innovate (like 3M and Google do), 6) Special circumstances (like Hack-a-thons at Facebook and others.)

- This is the time for what Linda Hill calls "Creative Abrasion" or collaborative problem-solving to co-create ideas.
- Develop minimum viable products/rapid prototypes.

Iterate

- Get responses from different users, peers, and others to your minimum viable prototypes.
- Modify and test again with what Hill calls "Creative Agility" or discovery-driven learning/testing.
- Get more responses from other users, peers and others.

Analyze

- Analyze, filter and decipher those responses as part of what Hill calls "Creative Resolution" or integrated decision-making and then

Implement and scale across products, processes, services, technologies and business models.

The Secret Sauce in a Best Current Thinking Approach to Problem Solving[35]

Roger Neill's "Best Current Thinking" approach to problem solving is a magic elixir that makes problem solving dramatically more effective by focusing attention on possible solutions. Roger first introduced me to his approach at a workshop he was facilitating years ago. I always thought it was an interesting process. As I've used it since then, I've learned just how powerful it is. The secret sauce is its leveling ability. It's a mindset change.

- When you give someone a recommendation or proposal, you're selling. They're buying. You're forcing them into an evaluative, yes/no mode.

---

[35] From my November 27, 2018 Forbes.com article, *The Secret Sauce in a Best Current Thinking Approach to Problem Solving*

- When you go to someone with your best current thinking about solving a problem, you're inviting them to collaborate with you to build on your thinking and solve the problem together. As Roger reminded me, this is forward-looking and positive, different than a "strawman," which can be treated much more negatively.

Don't get me wrong. Sometimes selling is good. But the most productive, most collaborative co-creation sessions I've seen over the past few years have included a problem owner sharing their best current thinking and then joining in the problem-solving process as an equal participant.

The core of the process laid out below includes identifying the problem, its owner and decision maker, that owner putting their best current thinking on the table for all to improve, and the group going through a disciplined process to solve that problem in collaboration with the problem owner.

For this to work well,

- The problem must be real, material and solvable.
- The problem owner must be confident enough to be open to input while retaining ownership of the problem (and solution.)
- Participating problem solvers must focus on the problem and solutions and not the problem owner.

The Best Current Thinking Problem (BCT) Solving Process

1. In the beginning, there is a problem. Identify the problem owner and decision maker, who may or may not be different people. Decide whether to work the problem as a group (or not.) If yes,

2. The problem owner shares their going-in perspective on the problem, context and best current thinking around potential options. (Ideally these will be shared before the problem solving session.)

3. Answer questions for clarification (to help people understand context and best current thinking, not for them to comment on or improve the thinking – yet.)

4. Highlight the most positive of the best current thinking contributing to making it work.

5. Identify the key barriers keeping the best current thinking from working. (Get all the barriers on the table at the same time before working any of them.)

6. Decide on the most important barrier.

7. Directed brainstorm on the most important barrier: WYDIS (What You Do Is) with all participating, including the problem owner – generally need 6-8 WYDIS.

8. Problem owner pulls together into a possible remedy to that barrier (testing.)

9. If the possible remedy is not strong enough, continue to work this barrier. If the remedy works, determine whether that is enough to solve the overall problem. If yes, move on to action steps. If not, work the next most important barrier.

10. Action Steps: Agree what will get done by when by whom now that this problem is solved – and make sure those things actually get done.

???

Boot Camp question for you to consider:

How do you improve your innovation process?

???

Who? – Not the Chief Innovation Officer[36]

The whole premise behind a Chief Innovation Officer goes beyond useless to completely and utterly counterproductive. If one person is in charge of innovation, everyone else are not. And they must be. Anyone not innovating is falling behind those that are. Darwin taught us that that is a bad thing. So: No Chief Innovative Officers. No distinctions between scientific, artistic and interpersonal leaders. Everyone is responsible for innovating, creating and leading.

From STEM to STEAM

At HATCH Latin America, Creative Coalition President, actor Tim Daly explained to me why this is so important. He was one of the "Innovators and Communicators" at a session with Obama in early 2009. As they discussed the STEM education initiative to boost science, technology, engineering and math, Daly asked, "Where's the A?" It's the arts that put engineering and technology in the human context. *"Arts are the emissaries and custodians of our culture."* Thus STEM became STEAM.

The argument for including arts in education is compelling. Daly shared some data:

- 70-80% of young people that get out of jail in Los Angeles go back. That drops to 6% for young people that take part in the "Inside Out" creative writing workshop.
- 30% of U.S. high school students drop out. But students who have taken art programs through middle school are three times more likely to graduate than the norm.
- When you factor in the costs of recidivism and failure, an investment in youth arts programs returns $7 for every $1 spent.

This is why Daly "became radicalized about the importance of arts and art education." As he puts it, science is "meaningless" without arts. Artists make people feel.

---

[36] Adapted from my March 16, 2016 Forbes.com article, *Why You Should Eliminate Your Chief Innovation Officer*

Daly led a breakout group at HATCH on arts and education. One of its ideas was how to move people's view of art from dangerous to irrelevant to being part of the answer. The idea was to involve all three of the different types of leaders the world needs: tapping the scientific leaders for the rational, data, value and brain science arguments, the artistic leaders for the emotional connection and stories, and interpersonal leaders to deal with the politics and business of getting funding and support.

No False Tradeoffs

Innovation is too important to be left to the Chief Innovation Officer. Everyone must innovate. Everyone must create whether they prefer connective, component or blank page creativity. Science is too important to be left to the scientists. Everyone needs to understand science, technology, engineering and math. And everyone needs to leverage their own artistic side to communicate facts in a way that taps into emotions and sparks value-creating behaviors.

However, as one Chief Innovation Officer[1] explained to me, when making a cultural shift, a Chief Innovation Officer "*can* be an effective catalyst for change, as long as that person's charter is to create the right conversations and underlying business processes that connect the appropriate functions in a powerful and integrated way."

Break the trade-offs with some good old-fashioned gap bridging.

1. Get everyone aligned around a shared purpose. Without a shared picture of your mission, vision and values nothing else is going to work. Determine where you are going to play and what matters and why.

2. Build a common understanding of the current reality. Take a cold, hard, dispassionate view of the facts around where you stand with regard to your customers, collaborators, capabilities, competitors and conditions in which you operate. Remember that adding constraints actually increases innovation.

3. Bridge the gaps. Work through and implement choices around how you are going to win, how you're going to connect and the impact you are going to have. This is where you mash up your scientific, artistic and interpersonal leaders so they can leverage their individual strengths and preferences to innovate, create and communicate together.

Words matter. So do eliminate Chief Innovation Officer titles to help inspire and enable everyone to do their absolute best together to realize a meaningful and rewarding shared purpose.

[1]Got comments on this from a number of people. One particular person, who shall remain nameless, wrote:

"First of all, a few areas of complete alignment:

1. Words *do* matter. Several years ago, many companies jumped on the "Chief Innovation Officer" bandwagon and created the role without much org design thought or clarity re: what that individual was supposed to do.

2. Everyone can and *must* innovate.

I think there's always a danger in folks being far too literal in interpreting senior leadership roles. For example:

- Chief People (or Talent) Officer (we *all* need to focus on engaging the hearts and minds of our people)
- Chief Financial Officer (we *all* need to have some level of financial/business acumen re how the enterprise makes money)
- Chief Information Officer (we *all* need to effectively deal with information from various sources on a daily basis)
- Chief Technology Officer (we *all* need some understanding of how the science and technology embedded in our offerings creates competitive advantage)
- Chief Design Officer (we *all* are designers if you believe that "Everyone designs who devises courses of actions aimed at changing existing situations into preferred ones" - Herb Simon, Nobel Laureate in Economics)

(As a side note, I encourage you to Google the Charlie Rose interview with Apple's Chief Design Officer, Jonathan Ive. Even though Apple is renowned for their design prowess and have a cadre of talented design professionals, they still need someone who will take accountability to lead the design discipline at Apple, make decisions, break ties, ensure they continue to recruit and grow great design talent, etc.)

I think one important distinction is that areas like HR, Finance, IT, R&D, and Design are *both* functions *and* activities. Innovation, on the other hand, is certainly a business-wide activity, but it is *not* a function.

If you're driving a culture change to re-emphasize innovation, appointing a Chief Innovation Officer *can* be an effective catalyst for change, as long as that person's charter is to create the right conversations and underlying business processes that connect the appropriate functions in a powerful and integrated way.

So, I like the provocative title of your post, but I think it's important to convey that there *is* a way to have a CINO that can be effective in an organization, and not simply the chief innovator for the company."

Systematizing Innovation[37]

Almost everyone accepts the importance of innovation. Why then do most organizations do it so poorly? That's because innovation is generally random, haphazard, one-off and outside the norm. Instead, make it systematic and part of your everyday culture.

Doug Hall is a master innovator, always innovating himself and helping others innovate. His book, *Driving Eureka: Problem Solving with Data Driven Methods and the Innovation Engineering System*" has easy to

---

[37] From my November 13, 2018 Forbes.com article, *How To Lead The Change From Haphazard To Systematic Innovation*

understand frameworks, processes and ideas. Additionally there are valuable tools and some of Doug's best stories.

The book's fundamental framework deploys:

- Blue Cards to focus your efforts.
- Starting with the customer problem as what matters and why.
- A "Meaningfully Unique" framework.
- Diversity of ideas to multiply your impact.
- A systemic process.

Blue Cards

Doug suggests using Blue Cards to charter teams. These lay out your purpose, what you see as the "very important" opportunity or system improvement, clarity on whether you're looking for "LEAP" or "core" innovation on a long-term strategic or project-specific basis, whether this applies to the entire organization or a specific division or department, your name for the effort, a narrative describing how you got here, the strategic mission, strategic exclusions (barriers), tactical constraints (like design, time, resources, investment, regulation,) areas for project exploration or long-term innovation.

Customer Problem

Doug has taken a classic positioning statement and repurposed it to help frame innovation efforts. The elements include:

- Customer and problem (think target)
- Customer promise (think benefit)
- Product/Service/System proof (think reason to believe)
- Meaningfully unique (dramatic difference)

Meaningfully Unique Framework

This is an evolution of the framework Doug has been using for literally decades.

Meaningfully Unique = [Stimulus mining / Drive out fear] raised by diversity of thinking

Doug's definition of meaningfully unique is that people will pay more for something.

Doug has been against pure brainstorming forever. He sees it has just sucking the useless stuff out of tired people. Instead, he suggests providing people stimuli to prompt new thinking through exploring, experiencing, and experimenting building off his early days of "creativity, stimulus and fun."

None of this works unless you can give people permission to innovate and remove their fear of failure, embarrassment of punishment.

And the value of diverse perspectives, people and ideas multiplies the impact of everything.

Diversity

One of Doug's favorite quotes through the years has been "In God we trust. All others must bring data." Data is an equalizer. Doing things like using Fermi Estimating (breaking an estimate into discrete, bite-sized parts) help remove fear and make it easier for diverse people to participate. There's much more to be said about the value of diversity. Lack of diversity is one of the main reasons why the highest performing teams always fail over time.

Process

A core tenet of Doug's Innovation Engineering System is an easy to follow process: Define – Discover – Develop – Deliver with Plan-Do-Study-Act cycles within it and a healthy dose of mind-mapping to keep things moving. Blue Cards charter groups that come up with ideas. Yellow Cards help groups track those ideas.

Yellow Cards include idea headlines, customer/stakeholder, problem, promise, proof, price/cost, raw math, death threats (to the idea), passion (why we care.) They clarify whether the idea addresses a LEAP or Core opportunity or system in line with the Blue Card used to charter the group.

In closing, Doug reminded me about the importance of "leadership's role in the process of enabling the system of development. Recall - 50%+ of value is lost during development. Simply telling people what to do - is not enough. Leadership needs to embrace a new mindset where they take responsibility for the systems of development. Command and Control and leadership by numbers needs to be replaced with "Commanders Intent" and systems that enable innovation by everyone. Only the leadership can do this - as only the leadership has the responsibility and authority for the whole."

Three Imperatives for Service Innovation[38]

Innovating in a service business works best if the innovations are: 1) aligned with your core purpose, 2) meet a future consumer need and 3) can be executed by your organization.

Noodles CEO Kevin Reddy explained this model to me and how it works at his organization. Since dining out is a truly discretionary expense for every one of Noodles' customers, it must deliver a superior experience every time every customer comes through its doors. Ultimately, we're all in service businesses so this applies to all of us.

Align Around a Shared Purpose

People in the organization must understand, believe and act on its core purpose. Reddy knows that any innovation and change must flow from, and contribute to, that core purpose, connecting with both current and new guests.

---

[38] From my February 20, 2013 Forbes.com article, *Three Imperatives for Service Innovation*

oodles' case this is about how it defines the dining experience, which Reddy summarized as: *"Really good food, served by genuinely nice people, in a friendly, welcoming place."*

Noodles differentiates itself by providing quicker service and a finer dining experience than other casual restaurants (though not as quick as quick serve nor as fine as fine dining). It is about delivering a superior dining experience at a great value in terms of financial and time costs.

Understand Future Consumer Needs

Innovation is forward looking. Solving yesterday's problems is important, but not innovative. Copying what others do well is often a good approach, but not innovative. Reddy suggests that innovation starts with knowing and believing in where consumer needs are going. Then creating a picture of what's important. Followed by *"inspiring and motivating people to embrace that vision."*

Thus, *"true innovation is about taking risk."* Reddy's steps are:

1. Choose the future consumer needs you are going to focus on
2. Create a picture of what success is
3. Get clear on the behaviors required to get there

Do the Doable

Armed with possible ideas, Reddy suggests the next step is *"Really understanding what our system can execute."* It's a truism that a good idea poorly executed is not worth anything. Reddy and his team make sure the ideas build on their core purpose, move the organization toward where consumers are heading and then make sure the whole organization:

1. Believes in and is passionate about the innovation
2. Is clear about how to bring the innovation to life
3. Has the training and tools required to execute

Reddy gave me a good example of a Noodles' innovation. Surprise. Much of the *"really good food"* Noodles serves is noodle-based. (Who would have thunk?) Consumers are valuing more and more ethnic variety in their food options. So ,Noodles is serving an increasing array of global flavors.

One option is Japanese Pan Noodles. It's a consumer-driven idea in line with Noodles' core purpose. But execution is key as there's a *"dramatic difference between getting it right and getting it almost right…with the consumer being really pleased and not happy."* Exactly three minutes is required to get the right caramelization. Fifteen seconds too little or too much doesn't work. Since Noodles is committed to going from order to delivery in five minutes, these 15 seconds count.

Japanese Pan Noodles work because they are in line with Noodles' purpose, meet an emerging consumer need and can be delivered well – as must your innovations.

CEO Discussion Points

CEOs main issue with regard to innovation is the conflict between trying to deliver near-term results while paving the way to long-term success. Almost by definition, investment in innovation has a short-term cost. Some CEOs ask people to innovate (and resource innovation) within their normal jobs. Some set up separate groups. Some accept that they're going to have to let others innovate and either fast-follow or acquire them. There is no one right answer.

"Have to eliminate the stranglehold of the few.

"Encourage innovation across the organization, including Finance and Contractors

"Make clear I am giving my "permission to explore" to the team.

Module 5: Communication

Everything communicates—everything you are, do and say, and everything you are not, don't do and don't say. It's generally not quite as stark as Lin-Manuel Miranda's *"Who lives who dies who tells your story"*. But you must decide if you are going to live and craft your own story or have others determine it for you. We suggest a BRAVE approach to scaling communication across Behaviors, Relationships, Attitudes, Values and the Environment from the outside in.

Environment - Where to play? (Context)

Leadership positioning guides how you'll influence your target audience. When evolving and scaling a culture from its current to desired state, expect contributors, detractors and watchers. Contributors want you to succeed. Detractors want you to fail. Watchers reserve their opinions. Some make decisions and some influence others. Even though implementers may not get a vote on the formal decision, they can veto it by not implementing it or change its effect by how they implement. And don't forget the influencers in the shadows.

How to Take Control of Your Own Leadership Positioning[39]

Everything communicates. Everything you say and do and don't say and don't do; and whom you say or do it to and when. Your personal leadership is going to get positioned in others' minds whether or not you plan for that to happen. For those that want to take control of their own leadership positioning, it starts with writing a positioning statement.

Leadership Positioning Components

- *Target:* Those whom will be impacted by your leadership.
- *Frame of reference:* The type of leader you choose to be.
- *Benefit:* How you will impact your target.
- *Reason to believe:* Why your target should follow you.

---

[39] From my December 13, 2017 Forbes.com article, *How to Take Control of Your Own Leadership Positioning.*

Target: Those whom will be impacted by your leadership

The best targets are both wide and deep.

Think broadly to include those you'll communicate with directly, those with whom they will communicate and all the influencers along the way. This could include peers, family and friends, associations, analysts, media, activists, competitors, collaborators, board members, shadow board members, shareholders, banks, regulators and government officials among others.

At the same time, dig deeply to understand your target's expectations, hopes and fears. Think about their context, what really matters to them, the occasions on which you can impact them and where you might connect.

Frame of reference: The type of leader you choose to be.

As mentioned before, world needs three types of leaders: artistic, scientific and interpersonal. Be clear on which you choose to be.

- **Scientific** leaders work on different problems, care about solutions and better thinking to connect with people's minds and impact knowledge.
- **Artistic** leaders work in different media, care about perceptions and new approaches to connect with people's souls and impact their feelings.
- **Interpersonal** leaders work in different contexts, care about the cause and rallying the team to connect with their hearts and impact action.

Many leaders blend different aspects of these three at different times. That often works well. For the purpose of this exercise, pick one of the three as your focus.

Benefit: How you will impact your target.

This is the pivot point of the whole exercise. Put yourself in the shoes of your target and answer the question "What does this mean for me?"

- If you're a scientific leader, this will most likely be about the types of solutions you help others get to.
- If you're an artistic leader, look at the type of feelings you want your work to engender.
- If you're an interpersonal leader, look at the purpose you're inspiring and enabling others to realize.

Reason to believe: Why your target should follow you.

Your followers won't believe what you say – unless it matches what you do and who you are. That's why it's generally stronger to craft your reason to believe in terms of be – do –say. Start by clarifying your own underlying beliefs. Then determine what actions you're going to take to communicate those beliefs. Finally, spell out the main message points that will make your target believe you.

From positioning to message

Don't confuse leadership positioning with message. Positioning is strategy. Message is implementation. One of my personal heroes is Charley Shimanski. Charley walked away from an investment banking career because he was personally driven to serve the underserved. I had the privilege of working with him at the Red Cross and at Rebuilding Together, helping the underserved stay in homes that needed repair.

I previously wrote about how Charley's messaging inspires others at the heart of the mission. Charley does as good a job as anyone at moving from positioning to message. He fundamental believes in his mission. That comes through loud and clear. He lives it every day. And then he finds way to make those following him feel proud about what they're doing. It's wonderful to watch.

Intuition versus being deliberate

This is yet one more example of the difference between intuitive and deliberate thinking per Daniel Kahneman. You can probably do a fine job trusting your intuition to craft your leadership message. Your intuition pulls together your experience and wisdom in a Nano-second. But if you want to increase your odds of getting your message right, take the time to think through your positioning and then build your messaging off that.

Other than hard-set detractors, people comply when aware of what they need to do. Indirect communication works fine here. Contribution requires understanding born of direct communication to allow for questions. People don't commit to leaders, teams or organizations. They commit to purpose and causes - to doing good for others. This involves going well beyond understanding to belief based on connecting at an emotional level with those who care most.

Dr. Bennet Omalu is a heroic scientific leader.[40] However, from a change management perspective, he spent years focused on the wrong people instead of those who care most.

In 2002, Omalu discovered chronic traumatic encephalopathy (CTE) during an autopsy of former Pittsburg Steelers' center Mike Webster. Repeated head blows had led to the deterioration of Webster's brain and his demise at age 50. Over the next several years, Omalu and others worked to bring this to the attention of National Football League leadership, culminating in a presentation to NFL Commissioner Roger Goodell at a league-wide concussion summit in 2007. There, the research was "dismissed."

Getting to Yes

Omalu was talking to the wrong people. The balance of consequences for league management favored protecting the NFL brand and its revenue stream over protecting players

---

[40] From My April 13, 2016 Forbes.com article *How NFL Concussion Fixes Were Delayed By Bennet Omalu's Failure to Ask 'Who Cares Most?'*

The breakthrough came when players and their families understood the findings and took up the cause. Not surprisingly they cared more about protecting their own and family members' brains than about the NFL brand and pushed the issue.

Eventually, in a <u>congressional hearing last month</u>, 14 years after Omalu's discovery, Jeff Miller, the NFL's senior vice president for health and safety was asked, "Do you think there is a link between football and degenerative brain disorders like CTE?" He replied, "Yes."

Start With "Who Cares Most?"

Revolutions aren't started by those reaping the rewards of the established system. They are started by that system's victims. The world's response to climate change is going to be led by the 500,000 people who, like the residents of Isle de Jean Charles, LA, are about to be displaced by rising sea levels. Changes to the U.S. healthcare system are going to be led by those unable to afford reasonable care. If you want real change, find those who care most. If no one cares enough, find something else to change.

This overriding question changes your approach to each of the other five BRAVE leadership questions: 1) Where to play? 2) What matters and why? 3) How to win? 4) How to connect? 5) What impact?

Where to Play to Benefit Those Who Care Most?

Move from a general perspective to what's most important in the context and environment for those who care most. Focus there. For Omalu this meant places in which football players banged their heads in practice or games.

What Matters and Why to Those Who Care Most?

People don't commit to leaders or organizations. They commit to causes, to doing good for others. Focus on what matters and why from the perspective of those who care most. For Omalu, these were football players' families.

How to Win with Those Who Care Most?

Strategy, posture and culture are about differential choices. Get clear on those choices on the way to delivering what matters to those who care most. For Omalu this was the best in class scientific revelation that 28% of professional football players were going to suffer from CTE unless things changed.

How to Connect with Those Who Care Most?

Almost by definition, a revolutionary message is not going to sit well with everyone. Don't worry about everyone. Worry about those who care most. Understand their platform for change, their picture of success and what they can do to move things forward. Build your message on that and deliver it to, with and through those who care most – like football families delivering Omalu's message to other football families.

What Impact on Those Who Care Most?

The first four questions are interesting but useless until you and your followers put things into action. Omalu's research was of no real value until people started changing habits and practices with a positive impact on those who care most. Focus on positive, valuable impact, otherwise you're just banging heads.

The world needs artistic, scientific and interpersonal leaders like Omalu. Interpersonal leaders can better help get the word out on artistic and scientific leadership by starting with the question "Who cares most?"

???

Boot Camp question for you to consider:

Who cares most?

???

Values - What matters and why? (Purpose)

Think about what matters and why on three levels: to you, to your organization, and to your audience. The closer these are aligned; the easier things will be. And root it all in "Be. Do. Say." If what you say doesn't match what you do, no one will believe you. If both don't match your fundamental, underlying beliefs, eventually they won't match each other. So, start with who you **be**. Then **do** things in line with those beliefs. Then, you deserve to **say** the words. Be. Do. Say.

???

Boot Camp question for you to consider:

What matters and why to those who care most?

???

Attitudes - How to win? (Choices)

It's often helpful to think through the platform for change, vision, and call to action to help you get at a core mantra. Then, fill that in with your master story/narrative and communication points all aligned with your personal brand. This becomes your message, building on one single core mantra, idea, guiding principle like "The People's Car" at Volkswagen. Part of this is positioning yourself as the chief enabler, enforcer, enroller, or experience champion in line with your organization's core strategy of design, produce, deliver, or service respectively.

TAI's Allen Schoer makes the point that CEOs need to be their organizations' narrators-in-chief. A narrator-in-chief is to stories like an editor-in-chief is to article submissions. The CEO owns the overall narrative, setting the context for others' stories. As Schoer puts it, "*Stories yield narrative. Narrative yields meaning. Meaning yields alignment. Alignment yields performance.*"

???

Boot Camp question for you to consider:

What are the core elements of your narrative?
(Mantra, idea, guiding principle, message points)

???

Relationships - How to connect? (Communication)

Since before Aristotle, leaders have known the importance of connecting with their audience on three levels. Aristotle called it Ethos, Pathos, and Logos. Some call it "Me. You. Us."

Start with Ethos - your competence, intentions, and the empathy you have with your audience. If you don't convey confidence (so people are prepared to believe you), warmth (so people feel good about you), and caring (so people know why you care about them), there is no next step.

Next up is Pathos or the feelings you engender in your audience. As the poet Maya Angelou put it, *"I've learned that people will forget what you said, people will forget what you did, but people will never forget how you made them feel."* Build on their hopes, needs and desires.

Finally comes Logos and the facts and evidence that will win over your audience – but only if you have delivered on Ethos and Pathos first. Your audience must believe in you and must believe you care about them, before they can hear your evidence.

???

Boot Camp question for you to consider:

What's the ethos, pathos and logos (me, you, us) of your own story?

???

Behaviors - What impact? (Implementation)

The proposed communication MAP follows the Hermann Whole Brain Model. While we all use our whole brains, different of us have different preferences. Some are more prone to thinking. Others acting. Some lead with logic. Others intuition. This graphic depicts leading with acting and intuition and then moving around the circle:

- Target: act/intuition
- Message: think/intuition
- Amplifiers: think/logic
- Perseverance: act/logic

all to impact the target

Think

Act

Logic Intuition
(Hermann Whole Brain)

Amplifiers - Amplifiers are people and tools to help spread your message. Who created the musical Hamilton? Lin-Manuel Miranda. And who else? (Tougher question.) And his team. He doesn't get there without Thomas Kail (Director,) Alex Lacamoire (Music Director,) Andy Blankenbuehler (Choreography,) or Ron Chernow (Book,) and others. The only thing leaders can do all by themselves is fail. Success requires a team. Driving your message requires allies and tools across all forms of media from direct one-on-one to mass to social and even dance.

Perseverance - Effective communication is not a one-time, but an all-the-time thing. Go beyond one-way communication to iterating conversations, listening carefully to learn, build and evolve as others move from comply to contribute to commit. Systematize communication, leveraging purpose (why,) frameworks (how,) and incentives (what.) As others pick up story lines, move from being the strategist to storyteller-in-chief to narrator-in-chief to leading co-creation. Strive for ongoing, iterative, community-building listening, learning, and conversations.

Boot Camp question for you to consider:

Who and what helps you amplify your story over time?

???

Two pictures of Vatican Square at the start of Pope Benedict and then Pope Francis' terms. What's different?

Social media has become part of how we communicate.

- First it was a less expensive way for companies to reach customers.
- Then it became two-way communication.
- Now it's about customer-customer and peer-peer communities.

You're going to be on social media. The only question is whether you're controlling your message or someone else is doing it for you.

???

Boot Camp question for you to consider:

Who's controlling your online presence?

???

Risk Management[41]

How many times must we learn the same lesson before we do something different? The world is a scary scary place to do business. There are risks all over the place from unseen hackers to known competitors to weather to regulatory changes to employee theft. The lesson is that every organization must take a comprehensive, top to bottom, strategic approach to risk management involving everyone in the organization.

RSM US LLP's Sudhir Kondisetty argued just this point forcefully and elegantly at the "Best Practices in Risk Management" workshop at the CEO Connection Mid-Market CEO Convention this year. He drove home the importance of a strategic approach to risk management. As he puts it, "Managing risk can only be successful it it's in every phase of your systems, policies and processes."

Three ideas: 1) Take a strategic approach to risk management; 2) Clarify roles; 3) Act appropriately depending upon the threat

1. Strategic Approach to Risk Management

Strategy is about the creation and allocation of resources to the right place in the right way at the right time over time. By definition, this means your strategies must be fluid. Every action has a reaction. Thus. your actions change the world and render your strategies out of date instantly. This is why you must adopt an observe - assess - plan - act - observe cycle.

---

[41] From my November 8, 2017 Forbes.com article, *Why You Must Take a Strategic Approach to Risk Management*

Observe, continually looking for risks across the Five Cs of Conditions, Customers, Competitors, Collaborators, Capabilities, The essential question is how you can best build and marshal your own and your collaborators' capabilities to serve your customers better than can your competitors in the conditions you all face. Some of the most important risks include:

- **Conditions**: country, political/regulatory, social, environmental, financial
- **Customer**: demographic, psycho-graphic, brand, reputation
- **Competitor**: market
- **Collaborator**: systemic
- **Capability**: leadership, team, technology, resource

Pay attention to what's going on, looking for changes in any of these factors or sub-factors. The questions to ask are "What's different?" or "What's changed?" Be comprehensive in identifying changes. Few people worry about small, white cigar shaped clouds on the horizon. No one who took place in the 1998 Sydney-Hobart yacht race will ever overlook one of those again as its appearance was the only early warning sign of the disastrous storm that hit on the second day of the race.

Assess the risk. Some small, white cigar-shaped clouds are just that, signifying nothing. Understand the risks and their implication. Are the risks major or minor, temporary or enduring.

Plan. That assessment informs your plans to act on the risks.

Act in accordance with your plans.

2. Clarify Roles

The board, CEO and operational group have different roles when it comes to risk management.

The Board is accountable for governance. It sets policies and must ensure the organization has the capabilities required for appropriate risk management. This may or may not include and Enterprise Risk Management system.

The CEO is accountable for execution. Hence the title Chief <u>Executive</u> Officer. They own the culture along with its biases, beliefs and filters and manages the observe – assess – plan – act cycle described above.

The Operations Group implements the plans. Beyond that, they must serve as the organization's eyes and ears and drive continuous improvement.

3. Act Appropriately Depending Upon The Threat

Not all risks are created equal. The Gore company used to look at risks and threats using a water-line analogy. Something that damages things above the waterline would be a minor risk. Something that puts a hole in the board below the waterline and can sink the boat (or organization) is major.

- **Minor change/temporary impact:** Control the damage while staying focused on your priorities.
- **Minor change/enduring impact:** Factor into your ongoing organizational evolution.
- **Major change/temporary impact.** This is a crisis or opportunity that must be managed. Deploy the incident management and response plan that you already have in place. (And have it in place ahead of time.)
- **Major change/enduring impact.** Hit a restart button at this major point of inflection, re-look at your critical relationships, and change your strategy, organization and operations all together, all at the same time.

Crisis Management[42]

With Boeing and its 737 Max we're seeing one more example of how not to manage a crisis. Through the years, many have done this well and less well. The common theme is that leading through a crisis is about inspiring and enabling others to get things vaguely right quickly, and then adapt along the way - with clarity around direction, leadership and roles.

This plays out in three steps of a disciplined iteration in line with an organization's overall purpose:

1. PREPARE IN ADVANCE: The better you have anticipated possible scenarios, the more prepared you are, the more confidence you will have when crises strike.
2. REACT TO EVENTS: The reason you prepared is so that you all can react quickly and flexibility to the situation you face. Don't over-think this. Do what you prepared to do.
3. BRIDGE THE GAPS. In a crisis, there is inevitably a gap between the desired and current state of affairs. Rectify that by bridging those gaps in the:

   - Situation - implementing a response to the current crisis
   - Response - improving capabilities to respond to future crises
   - Prevention - reducing the risk of future crises happening in the first place

Along the way, keep the ultimate purpose in mind. It needs to inform and frame everything you do over the short, mid and long term as you lead through a crisis instead of merely out of a crisis. Crises change your organization. Be sure the choices you make during crises change you in ways that move you towards your purpose and not away from your core vision and values.

---

[42] From my March 21, 2019 Forbes.com article, *Learnings from Boeing's 737 Max, Coca-Cola, and Procter & Gamble on Crisis Management*

Prepare in advance

- Establish crisis management protocols, explicitly including early communication protocols.
- Identify and train crisis management teams (with clear leadership and roles.)
- Preposition human, financial, and operational resources.

Note preparing in advance is about building general capabilities and capacity – not specific situational knowledge. For the most part, there is a finite set of the most likely, most devastating *types* of crises and disasters that are worth preparing for. Think them through. Run the drills. Capture the general lessons so people can apply them flexibly to the specific situations they encounter. Have resources ready to be deployed when those disasters strike.

Threats may be one or more of the following, often in combination:

- Physical (Top priority. Deal with these first.)
- Reputational (Second priority. Deal with these after physical but before financial threats.)
- Financial (Third priority)

Physical threats and crises may be

- Natural: earthquakes, landslides, volcanic eruptions, floods, cyclones, etc.
- Man-made: stampedes, fires, transport accidents, industrial accidents, oil spills, nuclear explosions/radiation, war, deliberate attacks, etc.

Reputational threats and crisis may flow from physical threats and crisis and how they are handled, or may come from: choices by you or others in your organization, outside interventions, sudden awareness of things already there, etc.

Financial threats come from disruptions in your value chain: supply or product or resources (including cash), manufacturing, selling/demand, distribution, service, etc.

Now, back to three things you should do to prepare.

Establish crisis management protocols. Lay out who's going to do what when in a crisis. In general, you'll want first responders to deal with immediate physical threats to people and property. They should i) secure the scene to eliminate further threats to others and themselves; ii) provide immediate assistance to those hurt or injured or set up a triage system to focus on those that can most benefit from help; iii) trigger your communication protocols.

There are two parts to your communication protocols. Part I protocols deal with physical issues. Part II deal with reputational issues.

Part I protocols spell out who gets informed when (with lots of redundant back-ups built in.) These should have a bias to inform more people faster.

Part II protocols are about formal, external communication. At a minimum, the one, single primary spokesperson (and back-up,) message and communication points should be crystal clear. Three over-arching ideas from the Forbes Agency Council's 13 Golden Rules of PR Crisis Management:

- Develop strong organizational brand culture to ward-off self-inflicted crises and be better ready to deal with others.
- Monitor, plan and communicate, ever on the lookout for potential crises. Then be proactive and transparent, getting ahead of the story and ready for the social media backlash.
- Take responsibility. Own your own crisis in a human way. Seek first to understand, avoiding knee-jerk reactions, apologize, then take action that helps, not fuel the fire.

Identify and train crisis management teams. Protocols are useless if people haven't been trained to apply them. Make sure your first responders are trained in first aid and triage. Make sure your communicators are trained in communicating in a crisis so people know whom to contact when and when to trigger crisis management protocols.

One of the learnings from the Boeing 737 Max crashes is that their crisis management protocols should have been triggered years ago. It seems that some knew there was a potential problem and chose not to deal with it.

Prepositioning human, financial, and operational resources. People need direction, training and resources. Make sure there's a site leader at each of your sites with access to cash. Make sure your first responders have working first-aid kits.

React to events

Our fight or flight instincts evolved to equip us for moments like this. If the team has the capabilities and capacity in place, turn it loose to respond to the events. This is where all the hard work of preparation pays off.

A big part of this is knowing when and how to react without under or over-reacting.

- **Someone was counterfeiting Coca-Cola fountain syrup.** The only differences between the counterfeit syrup and Coca-Cola's was an extra line on the package and the addition of preservatives. No risk to consumers. No reputational risk. Some financial impact. Choose not to react. Hired private investigators. Found the counterfeiters. Shut them down without anyone ever knowing. Well done.
- **Capper got out of sync,** shredding glass shards onto the lip of glass bottles. Clear physical risk to consumers. Shut down the capper. Recalled all product getting every bottle out of every vending machine within 48 hours. Well done.
- **Handful of school children got sick in school** after drinking Coca-Cola. Investigations indicated there was nothing wrong with the product so Coca-Cola did nothing. More children got sick. It turned out preservative from pallets on which Coke cans were stored reacted to the ammonia wash inside Coca-Cola vending machines leading to the illnesses. Classic under-reaction led to massive forced recalls, huge financial and reputational damage.

The story of Procter & Gamble's reaction to its New Orleans' Folger's plant getting destroyed by Hurricane Katrina is a model for how to over-react in the best possible way. Their essential steps included:

- Contacting every employee they could, eventually finding all 550 to be safe.
- Putting $5,000 into every employee's bank accounts immediately to help them deal with short-term issues no questions asked while continuing to pay everyone their full salary during the shut-down.
- Bringing 130 trailers and dining facilities and personal care products to the plant parking lot for temporary housing for those that needed it.
- Flooding the area with people (pun intended) to get the plant back up and running within three weeks.

Bridge the gaps

While first responders should react in line with their training, keep in mind that random, instinctual, uncoordinated actions by multiple groups exacerbate chaos. Stopping everything until excruciatingly detailed situation assessments have been fed into excruciatingly detailed plans that get approved by excruciatingly excessive layers of management leads to things happening too late.

The preferred methodology for what Harrald calls the "integration" phase is to pause to accelerate, get thinking and plans vaguely right quickly, and then get going to bridge the gaps with a combination of discipline (structure, doctrine, process) and agility (creativity, improvisation, adaptability).

Situational questions (Keeping in mind the physical, political, emotional context)

- What do we know, and not know about what happened and its impact (facts)?
- What are the implications of what we know and don't know (conclusions)?

- What do we predict may happen (scenarios)?
- What resources and capabilities do we have at our disposal (assets)? Gaps?
- What aspects of the situation can we turn to our advantage?

Objectives and Intent

Armed with answers to those questions, think through and choose the situational objectives and intent. What are the desired outcomes of leading through the crisis? What is the desired end- state? This is a critical component of direction and a big deal.

Priorities

The Red Cross provides relief to victims of disasters. In doing that, the prioritization of shelter, food, water, medicine and emotional support varies by the type of disaster. If someone's home is destroyed by a fire in the winter, shelter takes precedence. On the other hand, if a reservoir gets contaminated, the critical priority is getting people clean water.

These examples illustrate the importance of thinking through the priorities for each individual situation – and each stage of a developing crisis. The choices for isolating, containing, controlling and stabilizing the immediate situation likely will be different than the priorities for the mid-term response, getting resources in the right place and then delivering the required support over time. Those in turn will be different from the priorities involved in repairing the damage from the crisis or disaster and preventing its re-occurrence.

Get the answer to the question, "where do we focus our efforts first?" and the priority choices clear. And get them communicated to all, perhaps starting with a set of meetings to:

- Recap current situation and needs, and what has already been accomplished (What)
- Agree objectives, intent, priorities and phasing of priorities (So what)

- Agree action plans, milestones, role sort, communication points, plans and protocols (Now what)

Bridge the gap between the desired and current state.

Support team members in implementing plans while gathering more information concurrently.

Complete situation assessment and mid-term prioritization and plans.

Conduct milestone update sessions daily or more frequently as appropriate.

- Update progress on action plans with focus on wins, learning, areas needing help
- Update situation assessment
- Adjust plans iteratively, reinforcing the expectation of continuous adjustment.

Over-communicate at every step of the way to all the main constituencies. Your message and main communication points will evolve as the situation and your information about the situation evolve. This makes the need that much greater for frequent communication updates within the organization, with partner organizations and the public. Funneling as much as possible through one spokesperson will reduce misinformation. Do not underestimate the importance of this.

First officer Jeff Skiles was the "pilot in charge" of the airplane that took off, ran into a flock of birds, and lost both its engines. At that point, Captain Chesley Sullenberger chose to take over. With his "My aircraft", followed by Jeff's "Your aircraft", command was passed to "Sully" who safely landed the plane on the Hudson River. Only one pilot can be in charge at a time. Two people trying to steer the same plane at the same time simply does not work.

The same is true for crisis and disaster management. Only one person can be the "pilot in charge" of any effort or component at a time. A critical part of implementation is clarifying and re-clarifying who is doing what, and who is making what decisions at what point – especially as changing conditions dictate changes in roles and decision-making authority within and across organizations. Make sure the hand-offs are as clean as the one on Sully and Skiles' flight.

Bridge the gaps between desired and current response and desired and most recent crisis prevention (improving things and reducing risks for the future)

At the end of the crisis, conduct an after-action review looking at:

- What actually happened? How did that compare with what we expected to happen?
- What impact did we have? How did that compare with our objectives?
- What did we do particularly effectively that we should do again?
- What can we do even better the next time in terms of risk mitigation and response?

This kicks off preparing in advance for the next crisis.

How to Prepare Your Organization to Survive the Big One[43]

Hurricane Michael wreaked havoc on Florida's Gulf Coast, wiping out almost every structure in places like Mexico Beach. Left standing among the ruins was one house, the "Sand Palace." It had been designed to survive the big one. Learn from that design and make sure your organization is fit for your environment, has a strong foundation and fundamentals, and passes the cookie test.

As described in Architizer, the owners and architects of the Sand Palace made more expensive and less convenient design choices that made the house capable of withstanding Michael's fury as all around it failed.

---

[43] From my November 1, 2018 Forbes.com article, *How to Prepare Your Organization to Survive the Big One*

Fit for environment

- The house was raised on stilts so that storm surge could pass underneath.
- The stairway from the ground to the first floor and its surrounding walls were designed to break away in a surge without causing collateral damage.

Strong foundation and fundamentals

- The building sits atop pilings that are 40 feet deep.
- Walls were made of poured reinforced concrete.
- Steel cables travel from the girders above the pilings though the roof and continue down the back wall.

Passing the cookie test – choosing survivability over immediate gratification

- A proposed balcony on the east wall was removed at the design stage.
- Some proposed windows were replaced with concrete.
- The roof overhang was kept very small compared with adjacent properties.

The cookie test measures the differences between low delayers who choose to eat the one cookie given them immediately versus high delayers who choose the alternate option of waiting 15 minutes for two cookies. The applicability to your business is the choice between short term profit, speed, or expediency over longer term sustainability.

Fit for environment

Organizationally, you should certainly care about natural disasters. And you should care about the entire context for your operations across customers, collaborators, capabilities, competitors and conditions.

- **Customers**: Design your organization outside-in, starting with customers' needs. Make sure you are ready to meet their current needs and adapt to meet their future needs. Think about the first line customers you serve directly, their customer chain, end users, and influencers.
- **Collaborators** are critical parts of your ecosystem. Understand your suppliers, allies, government/community leaders and how they might surprise you.
- **Capabilities**: Make sure your human, operational, financial, and technical capabilities, and your key assets are always evolving to adapt to your changing context.
- **Competitors** are the storm surges that can wipe you out if you're not ready. Consider all of them, whether they are direct, indirect, or potential.
- **Conditions** Monitor social/demographic, political/ government/ regulatory, economic, and market changes, continually asking what? So what? Now what? to stay ahead of the next storm.

Strong foundation and fundamentals

Purpose.

I'm tempted to leave this section as that. One word. Purpose. Those of you that get it can move on to the cookie test section. For the rest of you, by purpose I'm referring to the combination of mission, vision and values. This is the one thing the ultimate leader of any organization cannot delegate. You have to own this because it is the foundation for everything else. Strong, surviving organizations align their people, plans and practices around a shared purpose. Others do not.

- **Mission**: Why we are here, why we exist, what business we are in.
- **Vision**: Future picture—what we want to become, where we are going – in which others can envision themselves.
- **Values**: The things you will not compromise on the way to delivering the mission and achieving the vision.

Get these right. They are your foundational fundamentals. Dig your pilings 40 feet deep if that's what's required to survive the big one.

The Cookie Test

Organizationally, the cookie test is an organization's ability to pick, play out and stick to a single over-arching strategy. Picking one single strategy and aligning it with one culture, organization, and way of operating seems riskier than keeping options open. But choosing to be best in class at one thing versus good enough at many can be the difference between success and failure. Pick one.

The big one is coming. Make sure your organization is ready.

???

Boot Camp question for you to consider:

How prepared is your organization to react to a crisis?

???

Press Interviews

While you should probably not be your organization's spokesperson in a crisis, you will be called upon to talk to the press in other situations. Some thoughts on dealing with that:[44]

If you concentrate on answering interviewers' questions in press interviews, you're putting your result in their hands. If you're lucky, their agendas match yours, leading to a happy result.

Don't do that.

Hoping for good luck is not a plan.

---

[44] From my January 8, 2019 Forbes.com article, *Make the Best of Press Interviews with Three Points*

Instead, concentrate on the three points you want to communicate and use interviewers' questions as cues to help you do that. Now you're in charge. And you make interviewers' job easier. Instead of piecing together stories from scratch, they can tell your story – with their perspective on it.

Next, take control of interviews. Time is on your side if you stay focused on what you want to communicate and you control the dialogue, just as it's on someone else's side if they control the dialogue.

I have done a lot of interviews through the years. I continue to be interviewed by others and to interview leaders for my articles - over 500 so far on Forbes.com. One of my guidelines is not to go into an interview until I am clear on the "slant" of the article if I'm doing the interview or the three points I want to make if I'm being interviewed by someone else.

And I'm generally transparent about my going-in point of view on the story. I've found it to be helpful because very few people look at interviews as win-lose propositions. Instead, they want to collaborate to craft a story valuable for the audience.

In many ways, interviews are moments of impact. Like all moments of impact, think through the prelude, manage the moment, and follow-up.

Prelude – Prepare in advance

Objective—Be clear on your single objective for each press interview. What do you want the outcome and impact to be? Think in terms of effect on the ultimate audience: what you want them to be aware of; what you want them to understand; what you want them to believe; what you want them to do. Secondarily, think through your "Hidden X" – how you want them to feel about you after they read, listen to or watch the piece.

Anticipate questions—Know the interviewer, the audience, and their interest factors (things like competition, conflict, controversy, consequences, familiar person, heartstrings, humor, problem, progress, success, unknown, unusual, wants/needs.)

Twitter is a fantastic tool for this. Almost by definition, journalists want people to read, listen to, or view what they create. So, many of them Tweet. It's astounding what you can learn about interviewers by reading their recent Tweets. In one case, I figured out that someone who was about to interview me was a rabid Philadelphia sports fan. Despite being a New York sports fan myself, I chose Philadelphia sports examples to illustrate the points I made to him. He loved it – as did his readers.

Approach—There are always different ways to get to your objective. Figure out the most appropriate approach for the interviewer and their audience. Think about this as a communication strategy. This will lead to:

Key communication points: Get clear on the three points you want to drive. This is the most important thing to do to allow you to do more than just answer questions (merely cues for your points.) If you take away one idea from this article it's this one. Going in clear on your three main communication points is the key to make the most of press interviews. These points need:

Support: Facts, personal experience, contrast/compare, analogy, expert opinion, analysis, definition, statistics, and/or examples.

Deliver

Be clear, concise, complete (do one thing well,) constructive, credible, controversial, captivating, correct (must correct significant errors on the part of interviewer or press.) Be yourself, liked, prepared, enthusiastic, specific, anecdotal, a listener, a bridge, cool.

Follow Through

Deliver on commitments you make to the interviewer. If you say you're going to send them more information, send it. Soon.

Afterwards, think through what worked particularly well and less well to improve for the future. Then leverage those insights as you prepare for the next press interview.

CEO Discussion Points:

Not surprisingly, the communication module sparks the most discussion and most commitment to change.

CEOs get that inspiring is about communication. But it's "Be. Do. Say." Communication. People will only listen to CEOs words if CEOs actions match their words. And if their actions match their words, but not their fundamental, underlying beliefs, they will get caught. Be. Do. Say.

I've organized the multitude of communication thoughts and comments along Prelude (to set the context,) Main Theme (headline message) – the heart of it all "Maria", Melody you can whistle – (3 main communication points) - "I just met a girl named Maria," Chords to accompany the melody (supporting points and documents), Arrangement to give it color and character (amplifiers, persistent efforts.)

That is a helpful way for CEOs to think about communication.

- Where play – context
- What matters and why – headline message
- How win – main communication points and support.
- How connect – amplifiers
- What impact – persistent efforts

Prelude (to set the context)

"Who cares the most? Look at strategy and positioning through that lens. Behaviors on the BRAVE model.

"Communication attached to who cares most. Work with people who are most committed.

"Will work to create emotional connections with what we do and how customer feels – which will help my people get aligned.

"Will be even more conscious about how I make people feel.

"Will get my heart and head in conversation – with leadership team.

"Will get our operations right before branding it.

"Create and communicate a differentiator in the posture of the company.

"Communication model: deciders, implementers, influencers, shadow.

"Communicate more about the cause and the framework in which operate.

"Will focus on the unmet needs as we look for adjacencies.

"Will spend more time on the long term.

"Relook at vision and mission.

"Going to pull up and drive the vision – versus staying down in the trenches.

"Going to focus on things I can do that others can't do: vision, cultivating strategy with our great crew.

"Will write brand promise statement.

"Think about how I want my audience to feel (not what I want to say). (Per Charley Shimanski story)

Main Theme (headline message)

"Will move people to commit to the cause versus the leader. This is a big idea. Will help employees commit to something bigger.

"Need to build more messaging around our cause. Less on what we do. More on the impact.

"Will define the message/make accessible to all constituents.

'This boot camp was a wake-up call that I wasn't behaving like me. I know the right thing to do. The message I send in my usual manner sets the tone I need to send. I know the impact of decisions on others. I actually stepped out (of the session) and moved on one issue. Differently tomorrow doesn't work for me. It's different in the next hour.

"Evaluate the word that I want the organization to be know by and myself included: "Trust". Makes sure everything we and I are doing is consistent with trust.

"Authenticity re: personal message.

"Focus more on message – how I can inspire.

"Knowledge is not the beginning of movement. Emotion is the beginning of movement.

"Don't get caught up in the what.

"What's inspirational about the what.

"Consistency of message – CEO in the middle of the organization up and down.

"(Will) think about my message relative to the audience – tailoring for audience segments.

"Want to re-craft future vision of the company.

"Tying vision to founder's legacy is key.

"Carry messages of "noble intent" and "BRAVE authenticity" to everyone. The deeper you can push that in the organization the better.

"Put a different lens on thinking about vision of the company. Intolerance of poor performance.

"Sharpen my message. Get more concise. Stay closer to the core of the message both internally and externally.

"Will remember that "everything communicates.

"Will get my executives on the line and move towards living in the future state.

"Be less subtle.

"Directors/owners must have consistency of message as well.

Melody you can whistle (main 3 communication points)

"Particularly struck by the discussion of my role as narrator-in-chief – will do better to curate the various stories at our upcoming annual meeting.

"Work on my master narrative.

"Theme of branding the narrative and how you're expressing yourself

"Storytelling. Telling the narrative. Amplifiers – perhaps some amplifying in ways not intended. My version or different versions. Particularly important with new companies (that we tuck-in to our existing businesses)

"Conversation re: what are story is going to be – the why.

"Will use the A x B x C > D framework. (The Platform for Change x Envisioning the Future x Call to Action must overcome inertia. These are The Three Essential Elements of Compelling Communication)

(For change to occur, A x B x C must be greater than D where:

A is the **Platform for Change** – Why <u>must</u> I do something different? (The starting point to break inertia)

B is **Envisioning** <u>a brighter future</u> – WIIFM (All benefits are emotional)

C is the **Call to Action** – What should I do (What I should do must make me feel important) and

D is Inertia

Mathematically, if any one is 0, the total is 0 and change does not occur. Which, of course, is what generally happens. People forget, don't deliver, or don't follow through on one of components.

The framework works with influencers as well. And as a leader of leaders, most of your communication will be influencing the influencers.

But, for influencers, the framework requires a twist: It's not just about the result of the change, but the change process:

Platform for change– Why <u>must</u> I get involved at this stage? (As opposed to waiting until the initiative has some momentum) – choose your target well: strong supporters

Envision a brighter future – Two parts to this: Part I is envisioning a brighter future for myself once the change is in place. Part II is envisioning good things for me as part of the change effort. (Many, including me, used to call this "vision". But "vision" is what the communicator sees while "envision" is what the person receiving the communication sees.)

Call to Action – Make me feel important as part of the change effort.

The point is that you have to get the equation right for all the people involved in the change. While you have to figure that out first, don't forget to think through the steps as you influence the influencer.

Chords (Supporting points and documents)

"The leader controls the energy in the room. I will be more aware of that tomorrow

"Will utilize more stories in my communication.

"Review the whole communication architecture and cadence.

"Remember after I say, "I love it", to ask "What do you need me to do.?

Arrangement (Amplifiers and persistent efforts)

"Must continue to reinforce vision and mission and values. I have an annual gathering of our leadership team and the next layer or management. I have to do more. I should own it, wear it and communicate it.

"Solidify our strategy re communication around our senior management team.

"Reevaluate communication mechanisms – especially with mid-level managers.

"Work on management communications – then drive through to the people in our plants.

"Have laid out the vision. Have not put in a cadence around how often and how to reinforce the message and measure how bought in people are.

"Got a good vision. Do town halls. Now need more frequent, two-way, rhythm – move with responsible speed – including board communication.

"Going to drive more clarity re the global organization. Sometimes as a CEO get too busy. This was a day of good reflections. Have to think big (we are big) and act small.

"Board members are customers too – cannot take them for granted

"Going to step back and be a better steward of our vision and values – they're solid. Need to step back and reinforce and ensure alignment – sometimes getting too much into the minutia

"Use pictures around the office to better connect employees with portfolio companies and better demonstrate firm successes.

"I got hung up on social media and communication. I have a strategy. I have focus. I haven't evolved it. Tomorrow – update it.

"Review communication activities.

"I'm going to do a social media audit.

"Check our communications through social media – take seriously.

"Will start using social media.

"Emphasized need to do even more with social media.

"Revisit what we're doing on LinkedIn

"Going to reach out and build my personal contact network.

"Will employee/deploy a communications manager.

"Google alerts (on myself and my company)

"Twitter.

"Communicate to employees – never enough.

"Pay attention to the influencer list in the company – meet with them.

"Our communication too traditional.

"Will use video more: weekly video message, "In the know" video.

"Virtual trade show.

"Will mingle streams of communication.

"Will change the way we manage communication.

"Will hire a social media analyst next week.

"Hire a coop web/communication manager.

"Like WOW program – hire a WOW manager/rewards to highlight weekly "WOWs"

"Leverage technology to improve internal communication.

"Like the ideas around the "Friday" message. Craft all week long, "I'm going to include in this Friday's message."

"Keep amplifying my message.

"In 2012 we improved our communications systems and styles. Today, need to do the at again. Not something you can stop.

"Communicate. Communicate. Communicate. Be more visible with employees, Board, public.

"It's the little things. Hand write notes to people. Write to consumer who email us.

"In terms of more general communication, participants sparked to. The bridge.

- "will use the bridge in answering questions.
- "will use the bridge in all my communication, being clear on my three points and bridging to them in interviews and panels and general Q&A's"

Note, "The bridge"

1) Answer the question asked (briefly)
2) Bridge to the point you want to make

Final thoughts

Brave leadership is about inspiring and enabling others to do their absolute best together to realize a meaningful and rewarding shared purpose.

So, in leading through a point of inflection, be good and brave. Be other-focused and leverage the BRAVE framework to help others be who they should be, say what they should say and get done what they need to get done, thinking in terms of these questions in general, with your board and other stakeholders, with your people, in leading innovation and in communication:

- Where to play?
- What matters and why?
- How to win?
- How to connect?
- What impact?

Acknowledgements

At the heart of this book are the frameworks and insights from CEO Connection's CEO Boot Camps. I'm grateful to all the CEOs that have attended these boot camps and shared their perspective. I'd call them each out by name except the Non-Disclosure Agreements everyone signs before each boot camp prohibits me from doing that.

PrimeGenesis' fingerprints are all over this book and its framework. In particular, Mary Vonnegut, Jayme Check, John Lawler, and Mark Anderson's, who have co-facilitated CEO Boot Camps, supported by all of PrimeGenesis' partners - past, present and future.

Other insights came from CEO Connection's team and various strategic partners through the years. It's an ever-evolving cast of characters, but need to call out CEO Connection's Kenny Beck, Sibson's Howard Fluhr and Dan Fries, Greenberg Trourig's Paul Berkowitz, and Korn Ferry's Joe Griesedieck in particular.

About the author

George Bradt has led the revolution in how people start new jobs. He and his colleagues accelerate transitions so that leaders and their teams fulfill their potential faster. After Harvard and Wharton (MBA,) George progressed through sales, marketing, and general management roles around the world at companies including Unilever, Procter & Gamble, Coca-Cola, and J.D. Power's Power Information Network spin off as chief executive. Now he is a Principal of CEO Connection, Chairman of PrimeGenesis executive onboarding, and author of six books on onboarding, 500+ articles for Forbes, and twelve musical plays (book, lyrics & music.)

Business books authored or co-authored by George Bradt:

- The New Leader's 100-Day Action Plan (John Wiley & Sons, 2006, 2009, 2011, 2016)
- Point of Inflection (GHP Press 2017-19)
- Onboarding: How to Get Your New Employees up to Speed in Half the Time (John Wiley & Sons, 2009)
- The Total Onboarding Program: An Integrated Approach (Wiley/Pfeiffer, 2010)
- First-Time Leader (John Wiley & Sons, 2014)
- The New Job 100-Day Plan (GHP Press, 2012)
- CEO Boot Camp (GHP Press 2019)

George can be reached at gbradt@primegenesis.com

References

Anderson, Mark, 2013, *The Leadership Book*, London, UK. Pearson

Bradt, George. 2011–2019 *The New Leader's Playbook*. Articles on Forbes.com.

Bradt, George, and Jeff Scott. 2019. *Point of Inflection*. New York. GHP Press

Bradt, George, Jayme Check, and John Lawler. 2016. *The New Leader's 100-Day Action Plan*. 4th ed. Hoboken, NJ: John Wiley & Sons.

Bradt, George, and Gillian Davis. 2014. *First-Time Leader*. Hoboken, NJ: John Wiley & Sons

Bradt, George, and Ed Bancroft. 2010. *The Total Onboarding Program*. San Francisco: Wiley/Pfeifer.

Bradt, George, and Mary Vonnegut. 2009. *Onboarding: How to Get Your New Employees up to Speed in Half the Time*. Hoboken, NJ: John Wiley & Sons.

Bradt, George, and Mary Vonnegut. 2012. *The New Job 100-Day Plan*. New York: PrimeGenesis.

Buckingham, Marcus, and Donald Clifton. 2001. *Now Discover Your Strengths*. New York: Free Press.

Campbell, Joseph. 1949. *The Hero with a Thousand Faces*. New York: Pantheon.

Covey, Steven. 1989. *The 7 Habits of Highly Effective People*. New York: Simon & Schuster.

Doran, G. T. 1981. "There's a S.M.A.R.T. Way to Write Management's Goals and Objectives." Management Review 70, no. 11 (AMA Forum): 35–36.

Groysberg, Boris, Andrew Hill, and Toby Johnson. 2010. "Which of These People Is Your Future CEO?" *Harvard Business Review*, November.

Harrald, John. 2006. "Agility and Discipline: Critical Success Factors for Disaster Response." *The ANNALS of the American Academy of Political and Social Science* 604: 256.

Heiman, Stephen, and Diane Sanchez. 1998. *The New Strategic Selling*. New York: Warner Books.

Hsieh, Tony. 2012. *Delivering Happiness: A Path to Profits, Passion, and Purpose*. Mundelein, IL: Round Table Comics.

Leitner, Jeff, and Andrew Benedict-Nelson. 2018. *See Think Solve*. Foosa.

Linver, Sandy. 1994. *Speak and Get Results*. New York: Simon & Schuster.

Lodish, Leonard. 1984. Class discussion.: University of Pennsylvania, Wharton School.

Schein, Edgar. 1985. *Organizational Culture and Leadership*. San Francisco: Jossey-Bass.

Senge, Peter, Art Kleiner, Charlotte Roberts, Richard Ross, and Bryan Smith. 1994. *The Fifth Discipline Fieldbook*. London: Nicholas Brealey Publishing.

Skarzynski, Peter, and David Crosswhite 2014. *The Innovator's Field Guide*. San Francisco. Jossey-Bass.

Smith, Bruay. 1994. *The Fifth Discipline Field Book*. Boston: Nicholas Brealey. Publishing.

Walker, Sam. 2018 *The Captain Class; The Hidden Force Behind The World's Greatest Teams*. New York: Random House.

52392157R00114

Made in the USA
Lexington, KY
13 September 2019